Study Guide to Accompany Neil J. Salkind's

Statistics for People Who *(Think They)* Hate Statistics

4 EDITION

Prepared by David Kremelberg

Los Angeles | London | New Delhi
Singapore | Washington DC

Los Angeles | London | New Delhi
Singapore | Washington DC

FOR INFORMATION:

SAGE Publications, Inc.
2455 Teller Road
Thousand Oaks, California 91320
E-mail: order@sagepub.com

SAGE Publications Ltd.
1 Oliver's Yard
55 City Road
London EC1Y 1SP
United Kingdom

SAGE Publications India Pvt. Ltd.
B 1/I 1 Mohan Cooperative Industrial Area
Mathura Road, New Delhi 110 044
India

SAGE Publications Asia-Pacific Pte. Ltd.
33 Pekin Street #02-01
Far East Square
Singapore 048763

Acquisitions Editor: Vicki Knight
Associate Editor: Lauren Habib
Editorial Assistant: Kalie Koscielak
Marketing Manager: Helen Salmon

Printed in the United States of America

Paperback ISBN 978-1-4129-0476-6

This book is printed on acid-free paper.

11 12 13 14 15 10 9 8 7 6 5 4 3 2 1

General outline:

- Chapter outline
- Learning objectives
- Summary/key points
- Key terms
- True/False questions
- Multiple choice questions
- Exercises
- Short-answer/essay questions
- SPSS Questions
- Just for fun/Challenge yourself
- Answer key

Contents

Chapter 1: Statistics or Sadistics? It's up to You

Chapter outline
- Introduction to Part I: Yippee! I'm in Statistics
- Why Statistics?
- A Five-Minute History of Statistics
- Statistics: What It Is (and Isn't)
- What Are Descriptive Statistics?
- What Are Inferential Statistics?
- What Am I Doing in a Statistics Class?
- Ten Ways to Use This Book (and Learn Statistics at the Same Time!)
- About Those Icons
- Key to Difficulty Index
- Glossary

Learning objectives
- Understand the purpose and scope of statistics.
- Review (briefly) the history of statistics.
- Introduce you to descriptive and inferential statistics.
- Review the benefits of taking a statistics course.
- How to use and apply this book.

Summary/key points
- Introduction to Part I
  - Statistics are used by researchers in a very wide variety of fields to study a great number of interesting problems, making sense of the large sets of data they collect.
    - Michelle Lampl, a pediatrician and anthropologist, has studied the growth of infants, finding that some infants can grow as much as one inch overnight.
    - Sue Kemper, a professor of psychology, has studied the health of nuns, finding that the complexity of the nuns' writing during their early 20s is related to risk for Alzheimer's disease as much as 70 years later in their lives.
    - Aletha Huston, a researcher and teacher, has found that children who watch educational programs on television do better in school than those who don't.
  - Statistics can be defined as "the science of organizing and analyzing information."
  - Statistics is used to make sense of often large and unwieldy sets of data.
  - Statistics can be used in any field to answer a very wide variety of research questions and hypotheses.
- A brief history of statistics
  - Far back in human history, collecting information became an important skill.

- Once numbers became part of human language, they began to be attached to outcomes. In the 17th century, the first set of data relating to populations of people was collected.
- Once sets of data began to be collected, scientists needed to develop specific tools to answer specific questions. This led to the development of statistics.
- In the early 20th century, the simplest test for examining the differences between the averages of two groups was developed.
- The development of powerful and relatively inexpensive computers has revolutionized the field of statistics. While it allows individuals to conduct complex and computationally intensive statistical analyses with their own computers, it also allows people to potentially run analyses incorrectly or lead them to incorrect conclusions regarding their results.
- Today, researchers from a wide variety of fields use basically the same techniques, or statistical tests, to answer very different questions. This means that learning statistics enables you to conduct quantitative research in almost any field.

- Why study statistics?
  - Having these skills puts you at an advantage when applying to graduate school or for a research or academic position.
  - If not a required course for your major, taking basic statistics courses sets you apart from students who don't.
  - A statistics course can be an invigorating intellectual challenge.
  - Having a knowledge of statistics makes you a better student as it will enable you to better understand journal articles and books in your field as well as what your professors and colleagues study and discuss.
  - A basic knowledge of statistics will put you in a good position for further study if you plan to pursue a graduate degree in the social or behavioral sciences, as well as in many other fields.

- Tips for using this book
  - Be confident: Work hard, and you'll do fine.
  - Statistics is not as difficult as it's made out to be.
  - Don't skip chapters: Work through them in sequence.
  - Form a study group.
  - Don't be afraid to ask your professor questions.
  - Do the exercises at the end of each chapter.
  - Practice, practice, practice: Besides the exercises, find other opportunities to use what you've learned.
  - Look for applications to make the material more real.
  - Browse: Flip through the future material and review chapters.
  - Have fun: Enjoy mastering a new field and acing your course.

Key terms
- Statistics: A set of tools and techniques that are used for describing, organizing, and interpreting information or data.
- Descriptive statistics: A set of statistical techniques and tools that are used to organize and describe data.

- Data, Data set: A set of data points (where one data point = one observation/measurement).
- Inferential statistics: A set of statistical techniques and tools that are used to make inferences from a smaller group of data to a larger one.
- Sample: A subset of the population. In statistics, it is often the goal to generalize findings from a sample to a population.
- Population: All the possible subjects or cases of interest.

Chapter 2: Means to an End: Computing and Understanding Averages

Learning objectives
- Understand averages, or measures of central tendency, one of the key components of descriptive statistics.
- Learn how to calculate the mean, median, and mode.
- Understand the distinction between these three measures of the average.
- Understand that the mean is very sensitive to outliers.
- Additionally, understand which measures of the average to use with different types of data.
- Learn how to use SPSS to calculate measures of central tendency.

Summary/key points
- Averages, or measures of central tendency, are used to determine the single value that best represents an entire group of scores. Popular measures of the average include the mean, median, and mode. More details regarding these measures are presented in the following section.
- The mean consists of the middle point of a set of values, while the median consists of the middle point of a set of cases, and the mode represents the most frequent value in a set of scores.
- Only the mode can be used when determining an average for qualitative, categorical, or nominal data.
- Likewise, the median and mean can only be used with quantitative data.
- The mean can be considered the most precise measure, followed by the median, and followed finally by the mode.
- For a sample statistic, Roman letters are used. For a population parameter, Greek letters are used.

- Average: The one value that best represents an entire group of scores. This can be the mean, median, or mode.
- Measures of central tendency: Another word for averages. As in the definition of the average, measures of central tendency consist of the mean, median, and mode.
- Mean: The sum of all the values in a group, divided by the number of values in the group.
  - The mean is sometimes represented using the letter M, and is also called the typical, average, or most central score.
  - The mean is very sensitive to extreme scores.
  - When calculating the mean by hand, computing the "weighted mean" can help save time when your data contains multiple instances of different values.
- Median: The midpoint of a set of scores.
  - The median is sometimes abbreviated as Med or Mdn.
  - To compute the median, list all the values in order, from highest to lowest or lowest to highest. Next, find the middle-most score. If you have an even number of values, the median is calculated as the mean between the two middle values.
  - Percentile points: These are used to define the percentage of cases equal to and below a certain point in a distribution or set of scores. A score at the 25th percentile means that this score is at or above 25% of the other scores in the distribution.
  - As the median focuses on cases, and not the values of those cases, it is much less sensitive to extreme scores, or outliers, as compared with the mean.
- Mode: The value that occurs most frequently in a set of data.
  - To find the mode, first list all the values in the distribution, listing each value only once. Next, count the number of times that each value occurs. The one that occurs most often is the mode.
  - If a set of values has more than one mode, the distribution is multimodal.
    - A distribution can even be multimodal if it has multiple modes which are very similar but not exactly the same (i.e., 15 of one category and 16 of some other category.
- Skew (verb): When your data contains too many extreme scores, the distribution of scores can become *skewed*, or significantly distorted.
- Data points: Individual observations in a set of data.

True/False questions
1. The mode and median are both averages.
2. The mean is very sensitive to extreme scores.

Multiple choice questions
1. Of the following set of values: 170, 249, 523, 543, 572, 689, and 1050, what is 543?
   a. The mean
   b. The median
   c. The mode
   d. The percentile

2. What is the mean of the following: 1501, 1736, 1930, 1176, 446, 428, 768, and 861?
   a. 1105.75
   b. 1018.5
   c. 428
   d. 1930
   e. 8
3. Your data set contains a variable on region of residence which contains the following possible responses: Northeast, South, Midwest, West, and Pacific Coast. Which of the following measures of central tendency should you use for this variable?
   a. The mean
   b. The median
   c. The mode
   d. The weighted mean
   e. Both a and b

Exercises

1. Calculate the mean for the following set of values: 25, 37, 53, 72, 76.
2. Calculate the median for the same set of values: 25, 37, 53, 72, 76.
3. Calculate the mode for the following set of values: 7, 7, 12, 15, 17, 19, 22, 25, 27, 31, 35, 42, 42, 47, 59.

Short-answer/essay questions

1. Review the following set of values: 12, 24, 37, 42, 55, 62, 72, 77, 246, 592. What would be the best measure of central tendency to use for this set of values? Why?
2. You just finished conducting a study on college students which contained a large set of questions on demographic information, including topics like the participants' gender, major of study in college, year in college (freshman, sophomore, junior, or senior), and race. What measure of central tendency should be used for these types of variables? Why?
3. In a survey which asked individuals about their favorite styles of music, 37 replied rock, 27 said they preferred pop music, 14 stated they liked classical music the most, and three individuals stated that they preferred opera. Based on this data, would be the mode? Why couldn't the mean or median be used?
4. You just took the GRE exam (in preparation for graduate school) and received a total score in the 98th percentile. Is this a good or bad score?

SPSS Questions

1. Input the following set of 25 scores into SPSS: 72, 13, 79, 76, 29, 8, 12, 27, 90, 72, 29, 40, 22, 45, 28, 50, 40, 84, 71, 14, 56, 46, 25, 28, 33. Use SPSS to calculate the mean, median, and mode. Now, go through the numbers yourself and calculate these averages by hand and make sure they match.

Just for fun/Challenge yourself

1. A set of five values was found to have a mean of 54.8. You know that four of the values are 24, 27, 53, and 68. What is the fifth value?
2. It is close to the end of the semester, and your goal is to get at least an A- (an average of 90) in your class. Each of your three exams is worth 25% of your grade, and your final is also worth 25%. You received an 87 on your first exam, an 88 on your second exam, and a 91 on your third exam. What is the minimum score (represented as a whole number) that you need to get on your final in order to get your A-?

Answer key

True/False questions

1. True. The mean, median, and mode are all different averages.
2. True.

Multiple choice questions

1. b. The median
2. a. 1105.75
3. c. The mode

Exercises

1. 52.6
2. 53
3. Modes = 7 and 42

Short-answer/essay questions

1. Based on this set of values, the best measure of central tendency would be the median. First, the mode is really only preferred in situations where your variable is qualitative or categorical (i.e., situations in which the mean or median cannot be computed). Secondly, the mean should not be used in this situation because you have two very high outliers, 246 and 592.
2. For these types of variables, you can really only use the mode. Since these variables are categorical/qualitative, it would be impossible to calculate the mean, and similarly, the median cannot be computed for variables of this nature.
3. Based on this data, the mode would be "rock music", as this was the most common category of response. The mean or median could not be used with this type of variable as it is qualitative, or categorical.
4. This score is very good: only 2% of people who took this exam did better than you did.

1.

Statistics

Var

N	Valid	25
	Missing	0
Mean		43.5600
Median		40.0000
Mode		28.00[a]

a. Multiple modes exist. The
smallest value is shown

Mean = 43.56, Median = 40, Modes = 28, 29, 40, 72

Just for fun/Challenge yourself

1. $\bar{X} = \dfrac{\sum X}{n} \Rightarrow \dfrac{24 + 27 + 53 + 68 + x}{5} = 54.8 \Rightarrow \dfrac{172 + x}{5} = 54.8 \Rightarrow 172 + x = 274 \Rightarrow x = 102$

2. $\bar{X} = \dfrac{\sum X}{n} \Rightarrow \dfrac{87 + 88 + 91 + x}{4} = 90 \Rightarrow \dfrac{266 + x}{4} = 90 \Rightarrow 266 + x = 360 \Rightarrow x = 94$

Chapter 3: *Vive La Différence: Understanding Variability*

Chapter outline
- Why Understanding Variability Is Important
- Computing the Range
- Computing the Standard Deviation
  - Why *n*-1? What's Wrong with Just *n*?
  - What's the Big Deal?
  - Things to Remember
- Computing the Variance
  - The Standard Deviation Versus the Variance
- Using the Computer to Compute Measures of Variability
  - The SPSS Output
- Summary
- Time to Practice

Learning objectives
- Understand what measures of variability are, how they are used, and how they differ from one another.
- Learn how to calculate the range, standard deviation, and the variance by hand.
- Learn how to use SPSS to calculate measures of variability.
- Understand the benefits of unbiased estimates.

Summary/key points
- Measures of variability make up another important component of descriptive statistics, in addition to measures of central tendency.
  - Variability is a measure of how much each score in a group of scores differs from the mean.
- Measures of variability include the range, standard deviation, variance, and mean deviation.
  - The range is the easiest measure of variability to calculate, but it is the most general. It should never be used alone to reach any conclusions regarding variability.
  - The standard deviation is the most frequently used measure of variability, and is a measure of the average distance from the mean.
- Both the standard deviation and the variance include the term *n*-1. Estimates in which 1 is subtracted from the sample size are called *unbiased estimates*, which are more conservative estimates of population parameters.

Key terms
1. Variability: The amount of spread or dispersion in a set of scores.
2. Range: The highest minus the lowest score. This is a very general estimate of the range.

- Exclusive range: The highest score minus the lowest score.
- Inclusive range: The highest score minus the lowest score plus 1.
3. Standard deviation: The average amount of variability in a set of scores, or a measure of the average distance from the mean. This is the most common measure of variability, but is also sensitive to extreme scores.
4. Variance: The square of the standard deviation. This measure is much more difficult to interpret than the standard deviation, which is why it is used much less often.
5. Mean deviation: The sum of the absolute value of the deviations from the mean divided by the number of scores. This calculation differs from that of the standard deviation.
6. Unbiased estimate: An estimate of a population parameter in which 1 is subtracted from n. It is considered to be a more conservative estimate.
   - Biased estimates can be used if you only wish to describe a sample, while unbiased estimates should be used when making estimates of population parameters.

True/False questions
1. Two sets of values that have the same mean must also have the same variability.
2. It is possible for two or more sets of values to have the same standard deviation and variance.
3. Before the standard deviation or variance is calculated, the mean of scores first needs to be calculated.
4. The standard deviation is sensitive to extreme scores, like the mean.
5. It is common for a set of scores to have no variability.
6. The variance is easier to interpret than the standard deviation.

Multiple choice questions
1. Which of the following sets of values has the greatest variability?
   a. 2, 2, 3, 3, 4
   b. 7, 7, 8, 9, 9
   c. 2, 3, 5, 7, 8
   d. 1, 4, 7, 9, 11
2. Of the following sets of values, in which of the four is the mean equal to the standard deviation?
   a. 2, 4, 6, 8, 9
   b. 4, 7, 8, 8, 12
   c. 0, 2, 4, 6, 13
   d. 2, 4, 5, 9 , 11
3. Which of the following sets of values has no variability at all?
   a. 10, 20, 30, 40, 50
   b. 2, 4, 6, 8, 10
   c. 0, 0, 0, 0, 5
   d. 8, 8, 8, 8, 8
4. What is the most general measure of variability?
   a. The range

b. The standard deviation
c. The variance
d. The mean deviation
5. You are conducting a survey, and you wish to use a sample of respondents in order to estimate population parameters. Which of the following should you use?
   a. Biased estimates
   b. Unbiased estimates
   c. Both unbiased and biased estimates.
6. Which of the following is correct?
   a. The range is typically equal to the mean.
   b. The range is equal to the square of the variance.
   c. The variance is equal to the square of the standard deviation.
   d. The standard deviation is equal to the square of the variance.

Exercises
1. Compute the range of the following set of scores: 214, 246, 379, 420.
2. Compute the standard deviation and variance of the following scores: 32, 48, 55, 62, 71.

Short-answer/essay questions
1. When and why are unbiased estimates preferred over biased estimates?

SPSS Questions
1. Input the following set of scores into SPSS: 68, 9, 17, 87, 19, 37, 66, 78, 33, 29, 33, 61, 3, 57, 50. Calculate the range, standard deviation, and variance of these scores using SPSS.

Just for fun/Challenge yourself
1. Calculate the mean deviation of the following set of scores: 23, 45, 57, 62, 88.
2. What are all the possible scenarios in which the variance equals the standard deviation?

Answer key

True/False questions
1. False. In fact, it is much more likely that these two sets of scores have different measures of variability.
2. True. This is possible, but it would be very rare. This would be the case only if the standard deviation and variance are both equal to 0 or 1.
3. True. The equation for both the standard deviation as well as the variance includes the mean, so this value must be first calculated before the standard deviation or variance is calculated.
4. True. Both the mean as well as the standard deviation are sensitive to extreme scores, or outliers.

5. False. It is extremely rare for a set of scores to have zero variability.
6. False. This is because the standard deviation is stated in the original units from which it was calculated, while the variance is stated in squared units.

Multiple choice questions
7. d. 1, 4, 7, 9, 11
8. c. 0, 2, 4, 6, 13
9. d. 8, 8, 8, 8, 8
10. a. The range
11. b. Unbiased estimates
12. c. The variance is equal to the square of the standard deviation.

Exercises
1. The range = 420-214 = 206.
2. First, $\bar{X} = \dfrac{\sum X}{n} = \dfrac{32 + 48 + 55 + 62 + 71}{5} = 53.6$.

   Next, the standard deviation =

$$s = \sqrt{\frac{\sum (X - \bar{X})^2}{n-1}} = \sqrt{\frac{(32-53.6)^2 + (48-53.6)^2 + (55-53.6)^2 + (62-53.6)^2 + (71-53.6)^2}{5-1}} = 14.8$$

   Finally, the variance $= s^2 = 14.8^2 = 218.3$

Short-answer/essay questions
1. Unbiased estimates are preferred in situations in which a sample is used in order to estimate population parameters. In these situations, unbiased estimates are preferred as they give you a more conservative estimate as compared with biased estimates. For example, in regard to the calculation for the standard deviation, by subtracting 1 from the sample size, the standard deviation is forced to be larger than it would be otherwise, giving you a more conservative estimate.

SPSS Questions
1.

Descriptive Statistics

	N	Range	Std. Deviation	Variance
var	15	84.00	27.51069	756.838
Valid N (listwise)	15			

Just for fun/Challenge yourself

1. Calculate the mean deviation of the following set of scores: 23, 45, 57, 62, 88. First,

$$\overline{X} = \frac{\sum X}{n} = \frac{23 + 45 + 57 + 62 + 88}{5} = 55.$$ Next, the mean deviation =

$$\frac{\sum |X - \overline{X}|}{n} = \frac{|23 - 55| + |45 - 55| + |57 - 55| + |62 - 55| + |88 - 55|}{5} = 16.8$$

2. For this to be the case, you would need the square of the standard deviation (i.e., the variance) to be equal to the standard deviation. In other words, you would need a number that does not change when it is squared. This leaves you with only two values: 0 and 1. The only two possible scenarios in which the variance is equal to the standard deviation is when both of these values are 0 and when both of these values are 1.

Chapter 4: A Picture Really is Worth a Thousand Words
<u>*Chapter outline*</u>
- Why Illustrate Data?
- Ten Ways to a Great Figure (Eat Less and Exercise More?)
- First Things First: Creating a Frequency Distribution
  - The Classiest of Intervals
- The Plot Thickens: Creating a Histogram
  - The Tally-Ho Method
- The Next Step: a Frequency Polygon
  - Cumulating Frequencies
- Fat and Skinny Frequency Distributions
  - Average Value
  - Variability
  - Skewness
  - Kurtosis
- Other Cool Ways to Chart Data
  - Column Charts
  - Bar Charts
  - Line Charts
  - Pie Charts
- Using the Computer (SPSS, That Is) to Illustrate Data
  - Creating a Histogram Graph
  - Creating a Bar Graph
  - Creating a Line Graph
  - Creating a Pie Chart
- Summary
- Time to Practice

<u>*Learning objectives*</u>
- Learn how to create visually appealing and useful representations of data.
- Review different ways in which data can be represented using tables and graphs.
- Be able to choose the best type of chart based on the nature of your data.
- Learn how to draw several graphs by hand, as well as how to create graphs using SPSS.

<u>*Summary/key points Widow/orphan?*</u>
- The two previous chapters focused on measures of central tendency and variability. This chapter expands upon this, illustrating how differences in these measures result in different-looking distributions.
- A visual representation of data can be a much more effective way of illustrating the characteristics of a distribution or data set as compared with numerical values alone.
  - Tables can be used to help illustrate the distribution of a variable.
    - Tables that were covered include frequency distributions and cumulative frequency distributions.

- Charts/graphs can be used to pictorially represent the distribution of a variable.
  - Charts/graphs that were covered include histograms, frequency polygons, column charts, bar charts, line charts, and pie charts.
- Skewness and kurtosis are measures which are both used to describe the shape of a distribution.
- It's easy to make a "bad" chart. Certain guidelines should be followed in order to make a chart that is easy to read and clearly illustrates what you are trying to show.

Key terms
- Frequency distribution: A method of tallying and representing how often certain scores occur. Frequency distributions generally group scores into class intervals or ranges of numbers.
- Histogram: A graphical representation of a frequency distribution, where the frequencies are represented by bars.
- Midpoint: The central point of a class interval.
- Frequency polygon: A continuous line that represents a frequency distribution.
- Cumulative frequency distribution: A frequency distribution that shows frequencies for class intervals along with the cumulative frequency for each.
  - Ogive: Another name for a cumulative frequency polygon.
- Skewness: A measure of the lack of symmetry, or "lopsidedness", of a distribution. A distribution that is skewed will have one tail that is longer than the other.
- Kurtosis: A measure which relates to how flat or peaked a distribution appears.
  - Platykurtic: A distribution that is relatively flat compared to a normal, or bell-shaped, distribution.
  - Leptokurtic: A distribution that is relatively peaked compared to a normal, or bell shaped, distribution.
- Column charts: A type of chart in which categories are organized horizontally on the x-axis, and values are shown vertically on the y-axis. This type of chart is used to compare the frequencies of different categories with one another.
- Bar charts: A type of chart in which categories are organized vertically on the y-axis, and values are shown horizontally on the x-axis in the form of separate, separated bars.
- Line chart: A type of chart in which categories are organized vertically on the y-axis, and values are shown horizontally on the x-axis, which are connected by one or more lines.
- Pie chart: A type of chart which illustrates the proportions of responses to an item as a series of wedges in a circle.

True/False questions
1. A bar chart tallies and represents how often certain scores occur in the form of a table.
2. Skewness is a measure of the central point of a class interval.
3. A frequency polygon can be defined as a continuous line that represents a frequency distribution.
4. When creating a graph, everything should be labeled, and it should only communicate one idea.
5. Graphs should contain as much text as possible.

1. This is defined as: "A measure of the lack of symmetry, or "lopsidedness", of a distribution"
   a. Skewness
   b. Kurtosis
   c. Mean
   d. Variance
   e. Median

2. This is defined as: "A measure which relates to how flat or peaked a distribution appears"
   a. Skewness
   b. Kurtosis
   c. Variance
   d. Mode
   e. Leptokurtic

3. A distribution that is relatively flat compared to a normal distribution is called...
   a. Skewed
   b. Platykurtic
   c. Leptokurtic
   d. Mesokurtic

4. When creating a graph, the ratio should be approximately...
   a. One to two
   b. Two to one
   c. Three to four
   d. Five to seven

5. When determining class intervals, you should aim to have about this many intervals cover the entire range of your data.
   a. One or two
   b. Five to 10
   c. 10 to 20
   d. 50 to 100

6. The largest class interval is placed here in a frequency distribution:
   a. The top
   b. The middle
   c. The bottom
   d. Randomly

7. When you want to compare the frequencies of different categories with one another, you should use a...
   a. Pie chart
   b. Line chart
   c. Column chart
   d. Frequency distribution

8. When you want to show a trend in the data at equal intervals, you should use a...
   a. Pie chart
   b. Line chart
   c. Column chart
   d. Frequency distribution

9. When you want to show the proportion of an item that makes up a series of data points, you should use a...
   a. Pie chart
   b. Line chart
   c. Column chart
   d. Frequency distribution

Exercises
   1. Draw a histogram using the data from the following frequency distribution:

Class Interval	Frequency
90-100	2
80-89	8
70-79	4
60-69	12
50-59	14
40-49	20
30-39	14
20-29	7
10-19	3
0-9	1

   2. Using the histogram you just created, now make this graph into a frequency polygon.
   3. Using the frequency distribution from question 1 in this section, add an additional column in order to make this into a cumulative frequency distribution.

Short-answer/essay questions
{Omitted}

SPSS Questions
   1. Create a histogram using the data from question 1 in the *Exercises* section.
   2. Create a pie chart using the following data: Roman Catholic, 12 respondents; Protestant, 20 respondents; Jewish, 2 respondents; No religion, 6 respondents; other religion, 9 respondents.

Just for fun/Challenge yourself
   1. Using the cumulative frequency distribution you came up with for question 3 under the *Exercises* section, chart the cumulative frequency data into a cumulative frequency polygon, or *ogive*.
   2. If a variable has a mean of 53, a median of 62, and a standard deviation of 4, what is its skewness?

Answer key

True/False questions
1. False. This describes a frequency distribution.
2. False. This describes a midpoint.
3. True.
4. True. These are good pieces of advice to follow when creating a graph.
5. False. Including too many words can serve to detract from the visual message that your chart should convey to readers.

Multiple choice questions
1. a. Skewness
2. b. Kurtosis
3. b. Platykurtic
4. c. Three to four
5. c. 10 to 20
6. a. The top
7. c. Column chart
8. b. Line chart
9. a. Pie chart

Exercises
1. Your histogram should look like the following:

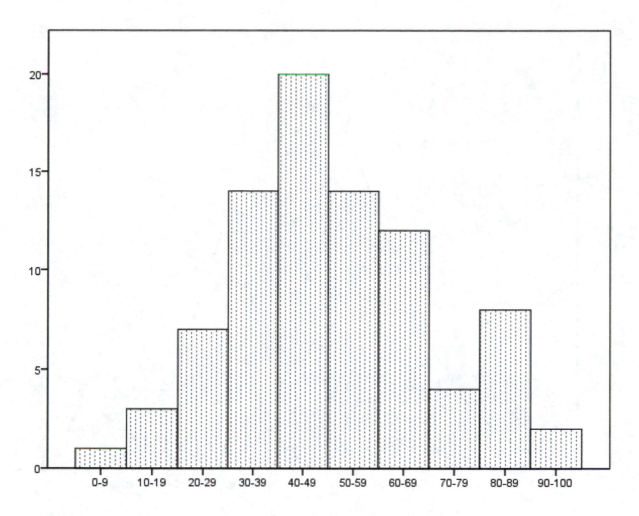

2. The frequency polygon should look like the following:

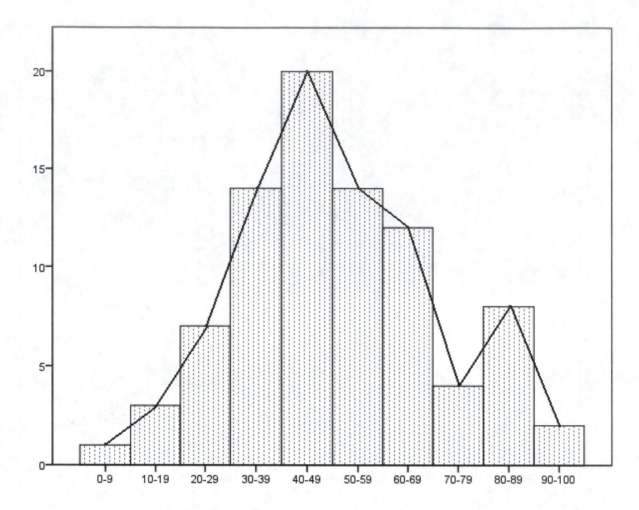

3. Your cumulative frequency distribution should look like the following:

Class Interval	Frequency	Cumulative Frequency
90-100	2	85
80-89	8	83
70-79	4	75
60-69	12	71
50-59	14	59
40-49	20	45
30-39	14	25
20-29	7	11
10-19	3	4
0-9	1	1

Short-answer/essay questions
{Omitted}

    1. See the *Exercises* section, question 1, for the correct histogram.
    2. The pie chart should look like the following:

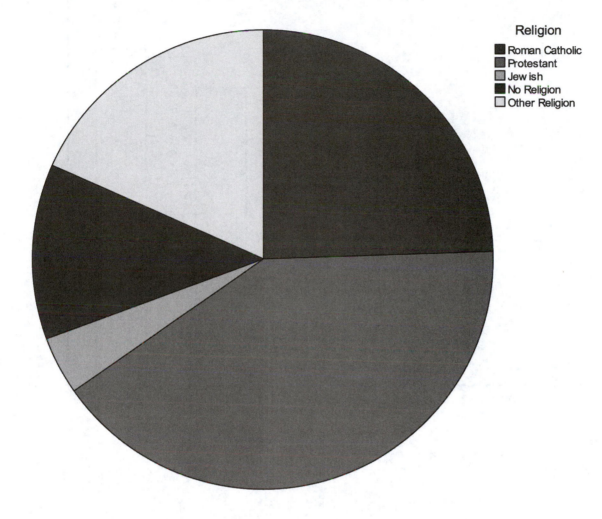

Just for fun/Challenge yourself

    1. Your cumulative frequency polygon, or ogive, should look like the following image.
        Drawing the bars can be helpful if done by hand, but is not necessary in an ogive.

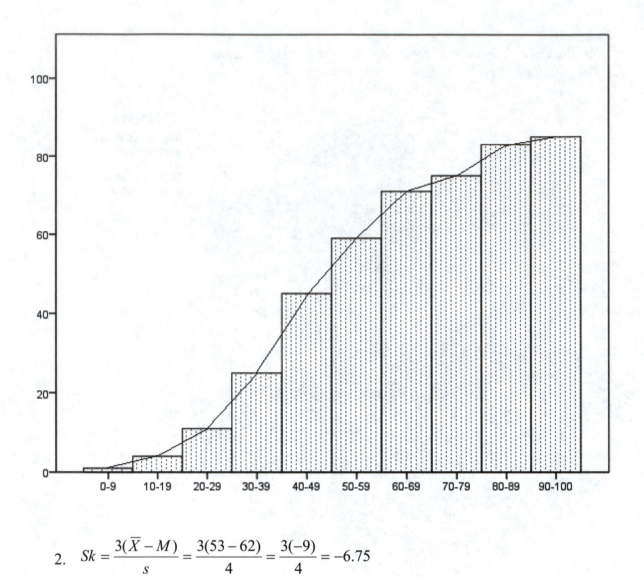

2. $Sk = \dfrac{3(\overline{X} - M)}{s} = \dfrac{3(53 - 62)}{4} = \dfrac{3(-9)}{4} = -6.75$

Chapter 5: Ice Cream and Crime: Correlation Coefficients

Chapter outline
- What Are Correlations All about?
- Types of Correlation Coefficients: Flavor 1 and Flavor 2
- Things to Remember
- Computing a Simple Correlation Coefficient
- A Visual Picture of a Correlation: the Scatterplot
- Bunches of Correlations: the Correlation Matrix
- Understanding what the Correlation Coefficient Means
  - Using-Your-Thumb Rule
- A Determined Effort: Squaring the Correlation Coefficient
- As More Ice Cream Is Eaten... the Crime Rate Goes up (or Association Vs. Causality)
- Other Cool Correlations
- Using the Computer to Compute a Correlation Coefficient
  - The SPSS Output
  - Creating an SPSS Scatterplot (or Scattergram or Whatever)
- Summary
- Time to Practice

Learning objectives
- Understand what correlation coefficients are used for.
- Learn how to interpret correlation coefficients.
- Be able to calculate Pearson's correlation coefficient by hand, as well as using SPSS.
- Be able to select the appropriate correlation coefficient to use depending on the nature of your variables.

Summary/key points
- Correlation coefficients are used to measure the strength, and nature, of the relationship between two variables.
- Pearson's correlation coefficient (r), which was the focus of this chapter, is used to calculate the correlation between two continuous (interval) variables.
  - Other correlation coefficients can be used when one or more of your variables are ordinal or nominal.
- When you have a direct correlation, both variables change in the same direction. With an indirect correlation, variables change in opposite directions.
- Correlation coefficients focus on generalities. This means that the correlation that you find describes the group, not every individual person in your data.
- The absolute value of the correlation coefficient reflects the strength of the correlation. Coefficients can range from -1 to +1, and the closer the absolute value is to 1, the stronger the relationship.
- The correlation between two variables will be reduced if the range of one or both of the variables is restricted.

- A scatterplot, or scattergram, can be used to visually illustrate a correlation between two variables. A positive slope represents a direct correlation, while a negative slope represents an indirect correlation.
- Correlation matrices are used in order to summarize correlations between a set of variables.
- The coefficient of determination is more precise than using a correlation coefficient alone, and is equal to the percentage of variance in one variable that is accounted for by the variance in a second variable.
- The fact that two variables are correlated does not imply that one causes the other.

Key terms
- Correlation coefficient: A numerical index that reflects the relationship between two variables.
  - Ranges between -1 and +1.
  - Also known as a bivariate correlation.
- Pearson product-moment correlation: A specific type of correlation coefficient developed by Karl Pearson. It is specifically suited to determining the correlation between two continuous variables.
- Direct correlation: A positive correlation where the values of both variables change in the same direction.
- Indirect correlation: A negative correlation where the values of both variables move in opposite directions.
- Scatterplot, or scattergram: A plot of matched data points. These are used to illustrate correlations between variables.
- Linear correlation: A correlation that is best expressed as a straight line.
- Curvilinear relationship: A situation in which the correlation between two variables begins as a direct correlation, then becomes an indirect correlation, or vice versa.
- Correlation matrix: A table of correlation coefficients in which variables compose the rows and columns of the table, and the intersections of the variables are represented by correlation coefficients.
- Coefficient of determination: The amount of variance accounted for in a relationship between two variables.
  - Equal to the square of the Pearson product-moment correlation coefficient.
- Coefficient of alienation (a.k.a. coefficient of non-determination): The amount of unexplained variance in a relationship between two variables.
  - Equal to 1 minus the coefficient of determination.
- Phi coefficient: A measure used to estimate the correlation between two nominal variables.
- Rank biserial coefficient: A measure used to estimate the correlation between one nominal and one ordinal variable.
- Point biserial coefficient: A measure used to estimate the correlation between one nominal and one interval variable.
- Spearman rank coefficient: A measure used to estimate the correlation between two ordinal variables.

True/False questions
1. If two variables are correlated, this means that one of the variables causes the other.
2. If your variables are found to be correlated, this means that this is true for the entire group of respondents, but most likely is not true for each individual case in your data set.
3. Arriving at a negative correlation is always a worse result than if you had found a positive correlation.

Multiple choice questions
1. The range for Pearson's correlation coefficient is the following:
   a. -10 to +10
   b. -5 to +5
   c. -1 to +1
   d. -100 to +100
2. Pearson's product-moment correlation can be used to calculate the correlation between these two types of variables:
   a. Two interval variables
   b. Two ordinal variables
   c. One nominal and one ordinal variable
   d. Two nominal variables
   e. All of the above
3. If one variable increases while the other decreases, you have this type of correlation.
   a. Direct correlation
   b. Indirect correlation
   c. Curvilinear correlation
   d. Leptokurtic correlation
4. If two variables move in the same direction (i.e., one increases as the other increases, and one decreases as the other decreases), you have this type of correlation.
   a. Direct correlation
   b. Indirect correlation
   c. Curvilinear correlation
   d. Leptokurtic correlation
5. Which of the following is the strongest correlation?
   a. -.15
   b. +.27
   c. -.70
   d. +.55
6. Which of the following is the weakest correlation?
   a. -.22
   b. -.78
   c. +.12
   d. +.89
7. Pearson's product-moment correlation coefficient is represented by the following letter:
   a. r
   b. p
   c. t

d. c

e. z

8. If you compute the correlation between two variables, and one of the variables never changes, you can be sure that the Pearson correlation coefficient is equal to...

    a. +1

    b. 0

    c. -1

    d. +.5

    e. -.5

9. If a correlation is computed between two variables, but the range of one of the variables is restricted, your correlation will be:

    a. Lower

    b. Higher

    c. The same

    d. 0

    e. +1

10. In a scatterplot, if the dots cluster from the lower left hand corner to the upper right-hand corner, this indicates that these two variables have this type of correlation.

    a. A direct correlation

    b. An indirect correlation

    c. A curvilinear correlation

    d. A bilinear correlation

11. View the following scatterplot. What is the best estimate of the correlation between these two variables?

    a. -.20

    b. +.55

    c. -.98

    d. +.90

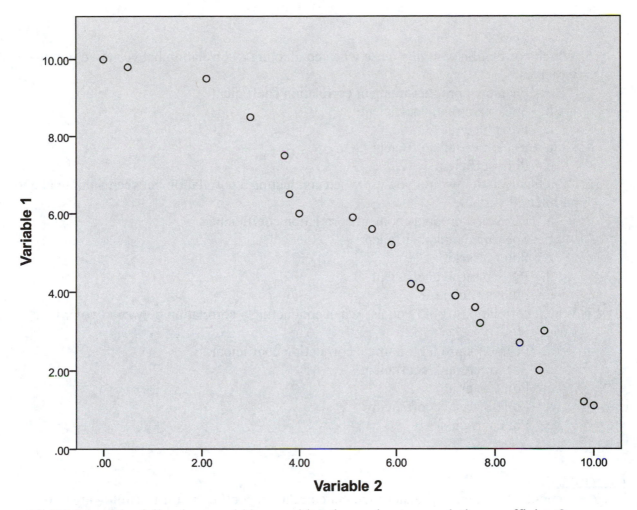

12. Which of the following would be considered a moderate correlation coefficient?
    a. .8 to 1.0
    b. .6 to .8
    c. .4 to .6
    d. .2 to .4
    e. .0 to .2

13. Which of the following would be considered a very strong correlation coefficient?
    a. .8 to 1.0
    b. .6 to .8
    c. .4 to .6
    d. .2 to .4
    e. .0 to .2

14. Which of the following correlation coefficients would indicate a weak or no relationship between the two variables included in the analysis?
    a. .8 to 1.0
    b. .6 to .8
    c. .4 to .6
    d. .2 to .4

e. .0 to .2
15. Which correlation would you use when conducting a correlation between two nominal variables?
    a. Pearson's product-moment correlation coefficient
    b. Spearman rank coefficient
    c. Point biserial
    d. Rank biserial coefficient
    e. Phi coefficient
16. Which correlation would you use when conducting a correlation between a nominal and an interval variable?
    a. Pearson's product-moment correlation coefficient
    b. Spearman rank coefficient
    c. Point biserial
    d. Rank biserial coefficient
    e. Phi coefficient
17. Which correlation would you use when conducting a correlation between two ordinal variables?
    a. Pearson's product-moment correlation coefficient
    b. Spearman rank coefficient
    c. Point biserial
    d. Rank biserial coefficient
    e. Phi coefficient

Exercises
1. Compute the Pearson product-moment correlation coefficient for the following two variables:

Years of Education	Income (000)
8	12
9	15
11	14
12	20
14	28
14	33
16	33
16	45
18	48
22	61
23	81

2. You find that the correlation between two variables is equal to +.76. First, judge the sign (+ or -) and strength of the correlation. Is it direct or indirect? Now, calculate the coefficient of determination and the coefficient of alienation. What do both of these values mean?

SPSS Questions

1. Input the data given for question 1 of the *Exercises* section into SPSS. Now, calculate the correlation coefficient using SPSS. Does your result match what you had calculated by hand?
2. Run a scatterplot using the same data. What does it show?

Just for fun/Challenge yourself

1. Describe a curvilinear relationship. Come up with an example of two variables that may have a curvilinear relationship, and explain why the relationship is curvilinear (use an example other than the one that was presented in the book).
2. If you are computing correlation coefficients between 10 variables, how many unique correlation coefficients will you have in total?

Answer key

True/False questions

1. False. Even if two variables are correlated with each other, this does not necessarily mean that one variable causes the other. The example presented in this chapter discussing the correlation between ice cream consumption and crime illustrates this possibility very well.
2. True. Correlations are conducted on your entire set of data: this means that while any correlations that you find are true for the entire data set, they're not necessarily true for each individual case or person. For example, if you found a direct (positive) correlation between years of education and income, this does not necessarily mean that all individuals with low education have low incomes (think Bill Gates). In practice, you will typically find some cases which go against the finding of the correlation.
3. False. A negative correlation, on its own, is neither any better nor any worse than a positive correlation.

Multiple choice questions

1. c. -1 to +1
2. a. Two interval variables
3. b. Indirect correlation
4. a. Direct correlation
5. c. -.70
6. c. +.12
7. a. *r*
8. b. 0

9. a. Lower
10. a. A direct correlation
11. c. -.98
12. c. .4 to .6
13. a. .8 to 1.0
14. e. .0 to .2
15. e. Phi coefficient
16. c. Point biserial
17. b. Spearman rank coefficient

Exercises

1.

Years of Ed	Income	X^2	Y^2	XY
8	12	64	144	96
9	15	81	225	135
11	14	121	196	154
12	20	144	400	240
14	28	196	784	392
14	33	196	1,089	462
16	33	256	1,089	528
16	45	256	2,025	720
18	48	324	2,304	864
22	61	484	3,721	1,342
23	81	529	6,561	1,863
Sum: *163*	*390*	*2,651*	*18,538*	*6,796*

$$r_{xy} = \frac{n\sum XY - \sum X \sum Y}{\sqrt{\left(n\sum X^2 - \left(\sum X\right)^2\right)\left(n\sum Y^2 - \left(\sum Y\right)^2\right)}} = \frac{11*6796 - 163*390}{\sqrt{\left(11*2,651 - 163^2\right)\left(11*18,538 - 390^2\right)}} =$$

$$\frac{74,756 - 63,570}{\sqrt{(2592)(51818)}} = 0.9652$$

2. First, this correlation coefficient was found to be positive, meaning that this is a direct correlation. This means that the two variables included in the analysis tend to "move together": in other words, as one variable increases, the other is expected to increase, and as one variable decreases, the other is expected to decrease. Next, as the correlation was found to be +.76, you could state that there is a strong relationship between these two variables.

Next, the coefficient of determination is simply calculated as the square of the correlation coefficient. In this example, the coefficient of determination is equal to .58. The coefficient of alienation is simply equal to 1 minus the coefficient of determination, or 1-.58 = .42. From the coefficient of determination, it can be said that 58% of the variance in one of the variables is explained by the variation in the second variable. Regarding the coefficient of alienation, this means that 42% of the variance in either of the variables cannot be explained by the other variable.

Short-answer/essay questions
{Omitted}

SPSS Questions
1. The following table presents the correct SPSS output. As you can see, the correlation coefficient matches the one calculated by hand.

Correlations

		Education	Income (1000s)
Education	Pearson Correlation	1	.965[**]
	Sig. (2-tailed)		.000
	N	11	11
Income (1000s)	Pearson Correlation	.965[**]	1
	Sig. (2-tailed)	.000	
	N	11	11

[**]. Correlation is significant at the 0.01 level (2-tailed).

2. The following figure presents this scatterplot. Based on the scatterplot, there appears to be a direct, or positive, and quite strong relationship between these two variables.

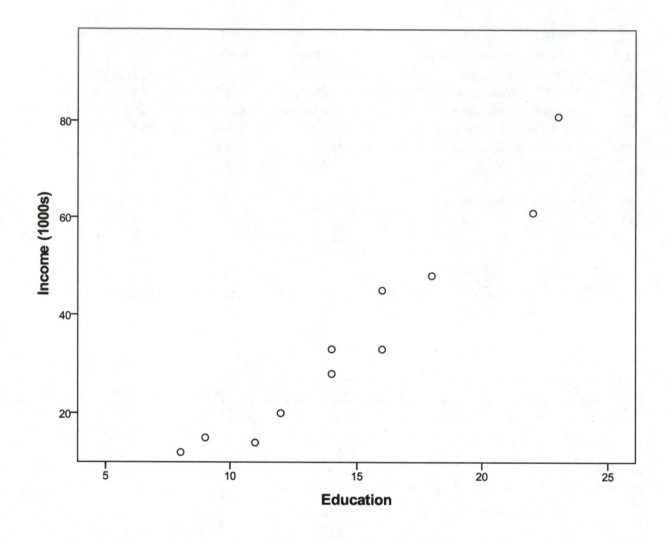

Just for fun/Challenge yourself

1. In a curvilinear relationship, the nature of the relationship between two variables substantially changes over the range of these variables. Specifically, a direct, or positive correlation between two variables becomes an indirect, or negative relationship. There are many possible examples, but one possible example could be the relationship between work satisfaction and hours worked per week. To illustrate, individuals who only work a few hours per week may be very dissatisfied with their work, as their income is very low and they're not able to work as many hours as they would like. However, individuals who work very long hours, for example 70 to 80 hours a week or more, may also be very dissatisfied with their work due to the large amounts of stress they experience and the fact that they have no free time. Individuals who work around a normal work week, 40 hours per week, could have the greatest levels of job satisfaction, as they are both making enough income and also have enough free time. If this relationship was plotted on a graph, it would be in the shape of an upside down "U": individuals with the fewest hours have the lowest satisfaction, then satisfaction increases as hours per week increase, up to the point of around 40 hours per week. Then, beyond this point, satisfaction decreases as hours per week continues to increase over and above 40 hours per week. When hours per

week is low, the relationship between these two variables is direct. However, when hours per week is high, the relationship between these two variables has become indirect.

2. This can be calculated in the following way:

$$Number\ of\ Unique\ Correlations = \frac{n(n-1)}{2} = \frac{10(10-1)}{2} = 45$$

Chapter 6: Just the Truth: an Introduction to Understanding Reliability and Validity

Learning objectives
- Understand the difference between reliability and validity and learn why they are important.
- Learn the difference between the different types of reliability and validity.
- Understand what steps you can take if you need to increase reliability or validity.
- Learn what measurement scales are and the differences between them.
- Learn how to compute and interpret different types of reliability and validity, both by hand and in SPSS.

- Before we start analyzing and interpreting data, it will be important for us to understand what reliability and validity are, as they both have very important implications regarding the data themselves.
  - Reliability explores the question: How do I know that the test, scale, instrument, etc. I use works every time I use it?
  - Validity explores the question: How do I know that the test, scale, instrument, etc. I use measures what it is supposed to?
  - If data are not reliable or not valid, then the results of any test or hypothesis will have to be inconclusive, as you are unsure as to the quality of the data themselves.
- A dependent variable is the outcome or predicted variable in an analysis, while an independent variable is the treatment or predictor variable in an analysis.
- Scales of measurement relate to the levels at which outcomes are measured, and consist of the nominal, ordinal, interval, and ratio levels of measurement.
  - The nominal level of measurement is the least precise, while the ratio level of measurement is the most precise. The "higher up" you are on the scale of measurement, the more precise, detailed, and informative your data are.
  - The more precise levels of measurement (for example, the interval level of measurement) contain all the qualities of the scales below them.
- Reliability relates to the degree to which a test measures something consistently.
  - Observed scores relate to the actual/measured score, while true scores relate to the score you would receive if the test contained no error.
    - The difference between these two scores is called the error score.
    - Observed scores may come close to true scores, but are rarely the same as true scores in the social and behavioral sciences due to the presence of error.
    - The less error you have, the greater the reliability.
  - Types of reliability include test-retest reliability, parallel forms reliability, internal consistency reliability, and interrater reliability.
    - Test-retest reliability is calculated as the correlation between scores from time 1 and scores from time 2, while parallel forms reliability is calculated as the correlation between scores from the first form of your test with the scores from the second form of your test.
    - Internal consistency reliability is calculated using Cronbach's Alpha.
    - Interrater reliability is calculated as the number of agreements between your two raters divided by the total number of possible agreements.
  - For high reliability, you want your reliability coefficients to be positive, and to be as large as possible (1 is the highest possible reliability coefficient score).
  - If your test is not reliable, you must try to lower your error. There are a number of possible changes that can be made for this purpose, including increasing the number of items or observations and deleting unclear items.
- Validity relates to the degree to which an assessment tool measures what it says it does.
  - Measures of validity include content validity, criterion validity, and construct validity.
    - Content validity is established by consultation with a content expert on the topic focused upon by your instrument.

- Criterion validity is determined by determining the association between the test scores and some specified present or future criterion.
- Construct validity is based on the judgment of how well a test reflects an underlying construct or idea.

Key terms
- Dependent variable: The outcome, or predicted variable in an analysis.
- Independent variable: A treatment variable that is manipulated, or the predictor variable in an analysis.
- Scales of measurement: Different levels at which outcomes are measured. The four scales of measurement are: nominal, ordinal, interval, and ratio.
  - Nominal level of measurement: The level of measurement where outcomes can only be placed into unranked categories.
  - Ordinal level of measurement: The level of measurement where outcomes can be rank ordered.
  - Interval level of measurement: The level of measurement where outcomes are based on some underlying continuum where it is possible to speak about how much more a higher performance is than a lower one.
  - Ratio level of measurement: The level of measurement where outcomes are based on some underlying continuum that also contains a true, or absolute zero.
- Reliability: The degree to which a test measures something consistently.
  - Observed score: The actual score that is recorded or observed.
  - True score: The true, or actual score that you would receive if a test measured your ability perfectly.
  - Error score: The part of a test score that is random and contributes to the unreliability of a test.
  - Test-retest reliability: A type of reliability that examines consistency over time.
  - Parallel forms reliability: A type of reliability that examines the consistency across different forms of the same test.
  - Internal consistency reliability: A type of reliability which measures the extent to which items on a test are consistent with one another and that they represent one, and only one, dimension, construct, or area of interest.
    - Cronbach's Alpha: A particular measure of internal consistency reliability.
  - Interrater reliability: A type of reliability that examines the consistency of raters.
- Validity: The quality of a test such that it measures what it says it does.
  - Content validity: A type of validity that examines the extent to which a test accurately reflects all possible topics and ideas under the subject or topic you are testing for.
  - Criterion validity: A type of validity that examines how well a test reflects some criterion that occurs in the present or future.
    - Concurrent criterion validity: A type of validity that examines how well a test outcome is consistent with a criterion that occurs in the present.
    - Predictive validity: A type of validity that examines how well a test outcome is consistent with a criterion that occurs in the future.

- o Construct validity: A type of validity that examines how well a test reflects an underlying construct or idea.
- o If a test or instrument lacks validity, changes can be made in order to improve validity, which will depend on the type of validity in question.
  - Content validity: Questions should be redone such that they are more consistent with what they should be according to an expert judge.
  - Criterion validity: You should re-examine the nature of the items on the test and question whether responses are expected to relate to the criterion you selected.
  - Construct validity: Review the theoretical rationale that underlies the test you developed.
- When working on a thesis or dissertation, it is strongly recommended that an instrument or text be used that has already been established to be reliable and valid.
- A test can be reliable and not valid, but it is impossible to have a valid test which is not reliable.
- The maximum level of validity possible is equal to the square root of the reliability coefficient.

True/False questions
1. Reliability and validity should be determined after an analysis is already complete.
2. The more precise levels of measurement (for example, the interval level of measurement) contain all the qualities of the scales below them.
3. If a test or instrument contained no error, then it could be said to have perfect reliability.
4. Observed scores are commonly exactly the same as true scores.
5. Smaller amounts of error are associated with greater reliability.
6. High reliability is associated with small reliability coefficients, as close as possible to -1.
7. If reliability is very low, nothing needs to be done. This finding would just need to be reported in your paper.
8. When working on your thesis or dissertation, it is to your greatest benefit to create your own test instrument.

Multiple choice questions
1. The manipulated treatment, or predictor variable in an analysis, is known as the following:
   a. The dependent variable
   b. The independent variable
   c. The correlated variable
   d. A skewed variable
2. The outcome, or predicted variable in an analysis is known as the following:
   a. The dependent variable
   b. The independent variable
   c. The correlated variable
   d. A skewed variable

3. Reliability serves to answer the following question:
   a. How do I know that the test, scale, instrument, etc. I use measures what it is supposed to?
   b. How do I know that the test, scale, instrument, etc. I use will work on all populations?
   c. How do I know that the test, scale, instrument, etc. I use works every time I use it?
4. Validity serves to answer the following question:
   a. How do I know that the test, scale, instrument, etc. I use works every time I use it?
   b. How do I know that the test, scale, instrument, etc. I use will work on all populations?
   c. How do I know that the test, scale, instrument, etc. I use measures what it is supposed to?
5. This is the level of measurement where outcomes are based on some underlying continuum where it is possible to speak about how much more a higher performance is than a lower one.
   a. Nominal
   b. Ordinal
   c. Interval
   d. Ratio
6. This is the level of measurement where outcomes can only be placed into unranked categories.
   a. Nominal
   b. Ordinal
   c. Interval
   d. Ratio
7. This is the level of measurement where outcomes are based on some underlying continuum that also contains a true, or absolute zero.
   a. Nominal
   b. Ordinal
   c. Interval
   d. Ratio
8. This is the level of measurement where outcomes can be rank ordered.
   a. Nominal
   b. Ordinal
   c. Interval
   d. Ratio
9. This is the most precise level of measurement:
   a. Nominal
   b. Ordinal
   c. Interval
   d. Ratio
10. This is the least precise level of measurement:
   a. Nominal
   b. Ordinal

c. Interval

d. Ratio

11. The actual, or measured score is called the following:
   a. The true score
   b. The observed score
   c. The measured score
   d. The error score
   e. The perfect score

12. The score that you would receive if a test contained no error is called the following:
   a. The true score
   b. The observed score
   c. The measured score
   d. The error score
   e. The perfect score

13. The difference between the score received if a test contained no error and the actual/measured score is called the following:
   a. The true score
   b. The observed score
   c. The measured score
   d. The error score
   e. The perfect score

14. Test-retest reliability examines the following:
   a. The consistency of raters
   b. The consistency across different forms of the same test
   c. The extent to which items in a test are consistent with one another and that they represent one, and only one, dimension, construct, or area of interest
   d. Consistency over time

15. Parallel forms reliability examines the following:
   a. The consistency of raters
   b. The consistency across different forms of the same test
   c. The extent to which items in a test are consistent with one another and that they represent one, and only one, dimension, construct, or area of interest
   d. Consistency over time

16. Internal consistency reliability examines the following:
   a. The consistency of raters
   b. The consistency across different forms of the same test
   c. The extent to which items in a test are consistent with one another and that they represent one, and only one, dimension, construct, or area of interest
   d. Consistency over time

17. Interrater reliability examines the following:
   a. The consistency of judges
   b. The consistency across different forms of the same test
   c. The extent to which items in a test are consistent with one another and that they represent one, and only one, dimension, construct, or area of interest
   d. Consistency over time

18. This type of reliability is calculated using Cronbach's Alpha:

    a. Test-retest reliability
    b. Parallel forms reliability
    c. Internal consistency reliability
    d. Interrater reliability

19. This type of reliability is calculated as the number of agreements between judges divided by the total number of possible agreements:
    a. Test-retest reliability
    b. Parallel forms reliability
    c. Internal consistency reliability
    d. Interrater reliability

20. This type of reliability is calculated as the correlation between scores from time 1 and scores from time 2:
    a. Test-retest reliability
    b. Parallel forms reliability
    c. Internal consistency reliability
    d. Interrater reliability

21. This type of reliability is calculated as the correlation between scores from the first form of the test with the scores from the second form of the test:
    a. Test-retest reliability
    b. Parallel forms reliability
    c. Internal consistency reliability
    d. Interrater reliability

22. This type of validity examines how well a test reflects some standard that occurs in the present or future.
    a. Predictive validity
    b. Concurrent criterion validity
    c. Criterion validity
    d. Construct validity
    e. Content validity

23. This type of validity examines how well a test reflects an underlying idea.
    a. Predictive validity
    b. Concurrent criterion validity
    c. Criterion validity
    d. Construct validity
    e. Content validity

24. This type of validity examines the extent to which a test accurately reflects all possible topics and ideas under the subject or topic you are testing for.
    a. Predictive validity
    b. Concurrent criterion validity
    c. Criterion validity
    d. Construct validity
    e. Content validity

25. If you need to improve content validity, you should do the following:
    a. Re-examine the nature of the items on the test and question whether responses are expected to relate to the criterion you selected.
    b. Review the theoretical rationale that underlies the test you developed.

c. Questions should be redone such that they are more consistent with what they should be according to an expert judge.
26. If you need to improve criterion validity, you should do the following:
    a. Re-examine the nature of the items on the test and question whether responses are expected to relate to the criterion you selected.
    b. Review the theoretical rationale that underlies the test you developed.
    c. Questions should be redone such that they are more consistent with what they should be according to an expert judge.
27. If you need to improve construct validity, you should do the following:
    a. Re-examine the nature of the items on the test and question whether responses are expected to relate to the criterion you selected.
    b. Review the theoretical rationale that underlies the test you developed.
    c. Questions should be redone such that they are more consistent with what they should be according to an expert judge.
28. Which of the following is correct?
    a. The maximum reliability is equal to the square root of the validity.
    b. The maximum validity is equal to the square root of the reliability.
    c. The maximum reliability is equal to the square of the validity.
    d. The maximum validity is equal to the square of the reliability.

Exercises
1. Say that you are very tired for an exam, and did much worse than you had anticipated, getting a grade of 72. If you had been wide awake and energetic, and if the test perfectly measured your knowledge, you would've gotten a 94 on the exam. What is your error score?
2. The following data illustrates a set of scores from eight respondents taken during two time periods. Calculate the test-retest reliability.

ID	Time 1	Time 2
1	72	76
2	54	43
3	86	92
4	92	94
5	99	87
6	43	69
7	76	43
8	84	92

3. The following data illustrates a set of scores from five respondents taken using two different forms of the same test. Calculate the parallel forms reliability.

ID	Form 1	Form 2
1	8.7	9.2
2	7.6	7.9
3	3.4	4.3
4	2.7	5.3
5	5.4	6.1

4. You and your friend, Robert, join a film club and over the course of a month, watch 10 films together. While you both have a similar taste in film, you don't agree on everything. The following data illustrates whether you and Robert believe these films to be good (G) or bad (B). Calculate the interrater reliability.

Film	1	2	3	4	5	6	7	8	9	10
You	G	B	G	G	G	B	G	G	B	G
Robert	G	G	B	G	G	B	G	G	B	B

Short-answer/essay questions

1. Come up with an example of an ordinal level of measurement. Now, what would be an example of an interval level of measurement?
2. Explain the difference between test-retest reliability and parallel forms reliability.

SPSS Questions

1. Input the data from question 1 under the *Just for Fun/Challenge yourself* section into SPSS and calculate Cronbach's Alpha. If you completed this *Challenge yourself* question, do the two figures match?

Just for fun/Challenge yourself

1. The following data presents scores for 10 individuals on a 5-item test. Using this data, calculate Cronbach's Alpha. Now, do a little additional research on Cronbach's Alpha. Is this score good or bad? Is it high enough to be considered acceptable?

ID	Item 1	Item 2	Item 3	Item 4	Item 5
1	8	9	7	8	8
2	5	6	8	4	5
3	1	2	1	1	1
4	4	3	4	5	4
5	1	3	2	3	2
6	5	4	5	6	5
7	2	3	4	2	3
8	9	7	8	7	9
9	6	5	8	5	6
10	4	5	5	4	5

Answer key

True/False questions

1. False. Reliability and validity should always be examined before an analysis is conducted. Otherwise, you risk having inconclusive results if the reliability and/or validity is not up to par.
2. True.
3. True. Error is measured as the difference between the true score and the observed (measured) score. If these two scores were found to be exactly the same, you would have no error, or perfectly reliability.
4. False. This is extremely rare in the social and behavioral sciences due to the presence of error.
5. True. The less error you have, the greater your reliability.
6. False. High reliability is in fact associated with high reliability coefficients, as close as possible to 1.
7. False. Having very low reliability is a serious concern. Depending on the type of reliability in question, the appropriate steps should be taken in order to attempt to increase the level of reliability.
8. False. Instead, it is to your greatest benefit to utilize a previously published test instrument whose reliability and validity have already been determined to be at least adequate. Otherwise, you run the serious and substantial risk of having your test instrument lack sufficient reliability and/or validity, which would call your data into serious question and force your results to be inconclusive.

Multiple choice questions

1. b. The independent variable
2. a. The dependent variable
3. c. How do I know that the test, scale, instrument, etc. I use works every time I use it?
4. c. How do I know that the test, scale, instrument, etc. I use measures what it is supposed to?
5. c. Interval
6. a. Nominal
7. d. Ratio
8. b. Ordinal
9. d. Ratio
10. a. Nominal
11. b. The observed score
12. a. The true score
13. d. The error score
14. d. Consistency over time
15. b. The consistency across different forms of the same test
16. c. The extent to which items in a test are consistent with one another and that they represent one, and only one, dimension, construct, or area of interest
17. a. The consistency of judges

18. c. Internal consistency reliability
19. d. Interrater reliability
20. a. Test-retest reliability
21. b. Parallel forms reliability
22. c. Criterion validity
23. d. Construct validity
24. e. Content validity
25. c. Questions should be redone such that they are more consistent with what they should be according to an expert judge.
26. a. Re-examine the nature of the items on the test and question whether responses are expected to relate to the criterion you selected.
27. b. Review the theoretical rationale that underlies the test you developed.
28. b. The maximum validity is equal to the square root of the reliability.

Exercises
1. Error score = Observed score − True score = 72−94 = −22.
2. The necessary calculations for this question are shown here. In essence, this question necessitates the calculation of the correlation between time 1 scores and time 2 scores.

ID	Time 1	Time 2	Time 1^2	Time 2^2	Time 1*Time 2
1	72	76	5184	5776	5472
2	54	43	2916	1849	2322
3	86	92	7396	8464	7912
4	92	94	8464	8836	8648
5	99	87	9801	7569	8613
6	43	69	1849	4761	2967
7	76	43	5776	1849	3268
8	84	92	7056	8464	7728
Sum:	606	596	48442	47568	46930

$$r_{xy} = \frac{n\sum XY - \sum X \sum Y}{\sqrt{\left(n\sum X^2 - \left(\sum X\right)^2\right)\left(n\sum Y^2 - \left(\sum Y\right)^2\right)}} = \frac{8*46930 - 606*596}{\sqrt{\left(8*48442 - 606^2\right)\left(8*47568 - 596^2\right)}} =$$

$$\frac{375440 - 361176}{\sqrt{(20300)(25328)}} = 0.6291$$

3. The following illustrates the calculations necessary to complete this question. In essence, this question requires the calculation of the correlation between form 1 scores and form 2 scores.

ID	Form 1	Form 2	Form 1^2	Form 2^2	Form 1*Form 2
1	8.7	9.2	75.69	84.64	80.04
2	7.6	7.9	57.76	62.41	60.04
3	3.4	4.3	11.56	18.49	14.62
4	2.7	5.3	7.29	28.09	14.31
5	5.4	6.1	29.16	37.21	32.94
Sum:	27.8	32.8	181.46	230.84	201.95

$$r_{xy} = \frac{n\sum XY - \sum X \sum Y}{\sqrt{\left(n\sum X^2 - \left(\sum X\right)^2\right)\left(n\sum Y^2 - \left(\sum Y\right)^2\right)}} = \frac{5*201.95 - 27.8*32.8}{\sqrt{\left(5*181.46 - 27.8^2\right)\left(5*230.84 - 32.8^2\right)}} =$$

$$\frac{1009.75 - 911.84}{\sqrt{(134.46)(78.36)}} = 0.9539$$

4. The following illustrates the calculation of the interrater reliability for this question. This calculation simply consists of the number of total agreements divided by the number of total possible agreements.

Film	1	2	3	4	5	6	7	8	9	10
You	G	B	G	G	G	B	G	G	B	G
Robert	G	G	B	G	G	B	G	G	B	B

$$Interrater\ Reliability = \frac{n\ Agreements}{n\ Possible\ Agreements} = \frac{7}{10} = 0.7$$

Short-answer/essay questions

1. An example of an ordinal level of measurement would consist of any variable which is categorical (consisting of a number of discrete categories) which can be ordered, or ranked. Some examples include highest degree earned, social class, and letter grade. An example of an interval level of measurement would consist of any variable which is continuous, but does not have an absolute or true zero. Some examples would include IQ, height, weight, and grade on an exam (in these examples, it is assumed that there is no "true" zero).

2. Test-retest reliability measures reliability, or consistency over time, while parallel forms reliability examines the consistency across multiple forms of the same test. Test-retest reliability would be calculated by determining the correlation between a test given at one time period and the test given at a second time period, while parallel forms reliability

would be calculated by determining the correlation between the two separate administrations of the test instrument.

SPSS Questions

1. The corresponding SPSS output for this analysis is presented below. The calculated Cronbach's Alpha score in this analysis was calculated as 0.969, which is identical to the figure you would have arrived at if you also calculated this by hand.

Case Processing Summary

		N	%
Cases	Valid	10	100.0
	Excluded[a]	0	.0
	Total	10	100.0

a. Listwise deletion based on all variables in the procedure.

Reliability Statistics

Cronbach's Alpha	N of Items
.969	5

Just for fun/Challenge yourself

1. First, the variances for all five items as well as the variance for total score needs to be calculated. As this calculation was covered earlier, it is not repeated here. The final column of the following table illustrates the correct values for the variances of each of the five individual items as well as the variance for total score.

ID	Item 1	Item 2	Item 3	Item 4	Item 5	Total
1	8	9	7	8	8	40
2	5	6	8	4	5	28
3	1	2	1	1	1	6
4	4	3	4	5	4	20
5	1	3	2	3	2	11
6	5	4	5	6	5	25
7	2	3	4	2	3	14
8	9	7	8	7	9	40
9	6	5	8	5	6	30
10	4	5	5	4	5	23
Variance:	7.39	4.68	6.40	4.72	6.18	130.46

Next, the variances for the five individual items need to be summed.

Sum of item variances = 29.37

Finally, the following equation presents the calculation for Cronbach's Alpha.

$$\alpha = \left(\frac{k}{k-1}\right)\left(\frac{s_y^2 - \sum s_i^2}{s_y^2}\right) = \left(\frac{5}{5-1}\right)\left(\frac{130.46 - 29.37}{130.46}\right) = 0.9686$$

These five items had a Cronbach's Alpha score of 0.9686. Generally, alpha scores of 0.7 or higher are considered acceptable. This indicates that these five items have a very high and very acceptable alpha score.

Chapter 7: Hypotheticals and You: Testing Your Questions

Chapter outline
- So You Want to Be a Scientist...
  - Samples and Populations
- The Null Hypothesis
  - The Purposes of the Null Hypothesis
- The Research Hypothesis
  - The Nondirectional Research Hypothesis
  - The Directional Research Hypothesis
  - Some Differences between the Null Hypothesis and the Research Hypothesis
- What Makes a Good Hypothesis?
- Summary
- Time to Practice

Learning objectives
- Learn the differences between a sample and a population, and how each is related to your research.
- Understand the difference between null and research hypotheses, as well as directional and nondirectional hypotheses.
- Learn how to create good hypotheses.

Summary/key points
- A hypothesis is an "educated guess" which describes the relationship between variables. In essence, it is like a more specific, directly testable version of a research question.
- In a study, a sample is drawn from a larger population and analyses are conducted on the sample itself. Optimally, it is possible to generalize your results to the population.
  - Hypothesis testing relates to the sample itself, not the population.
  - A *representative* sample must be used if you wish to generalize the results of your analyses to the population at large. Individuals in a representative sample should match as closely as possible to the characteristics of the population (while there are also more specific methodological requirements).
- Sampling error relates to how well a sample approximates the characteristics of a population.
  - Higher sampling error means a greater difference between the sample statistic and the population parameter, meaning that it is more difficult for you to generalize your results to that of the population.
- The two types of hypotheses are the null and alternative hypothesis.
  - The null hypothesis is formulated first and states that there is no relationship between your variables.
  - The research hypothesis, formulated second, states that there is a relationship between your variables.

- A research hypothesis that suggests the direction of the relationship is called a *directional* hypothesis. One-tailed tests can be used with these hypotheses.
- A research hypothesis that does not suggest the direction of the relationship is called a nondirectional hypothesis. Two-tailed tests should be used with these hypotheses.
    - Unless you have sufficient evidence otherwise, you must assume that the null hypothesis is true.
    - Null hypotheses always refer to the population, while research hypotheses always refer to the sample. Therefore, the null hypothesis is only indirectly tested (making it an *implied* hypothesis), while the research hypothesis can be tested directly.
    - While null hypotheses are written using Greek symbols, research hypotheses are written using Roman symbols (letters from the English alphabet).
    - Good hypotheses have the following features:
        - They are stated in declarative form, not as a question.
        - They posit an expected relationship between variables.
        - They reflect the theory or literature on which they are based.
        - There are brief and to the point.
        - They are testable hypotheses.

Key terms

- Hypothesis: An "educated guess" describing the relationship between two or more variables.
- Population: A larger group of respondents from whom a sample is collected, and which you hope to generalize to after conducting your analyses.
- Sample: A subset taken from a population for the purposes of your study. Data is collected on a sample, while the results are optimally generalized to the population.
- Sampling error: The difference between sample and population values.
- Null hypothesis: A statement of equality between sets of variables.
- Research hypothesis: A statement that there is a relationship between variables.
- Nondirectional research hypothesis: A hypothesis that reflects a difference between groups, but does not specify the direction of the difference.
- Directional research hypothesis: A hypothesis that reflects a difference between groups and also specifies the direction of the difference.
- One-tailed test: A directional test, which reflects a directional hypothesis.
- Two-tailed test: A nondirectional test, which reflects a nondirectional hypothesis.

True/False questions

1. A research question is a more specific, testable version of a hypothesis.
2. The null hypothesis is only indirectly tested, making it an implied hypothesis.
3. Good hypotheses should be (along with other attributes) brief and to the point, testable, and stated in declarative form.

Multiple choice questions
1. When conducting a study, you draw a smaller _____ from a larger _____.
   a. population; sample
   b. sample; population
   c. null hypothesis; research hypothesis
   d. nondirectional hypothesis; directional hypothesis
2. In order to generalize your results, you need to have this:
   a. A representative sample
   b. A representative population
   c. A population larger than your sample
   d. A null hypothesis
3. A representative sample should have the following:
   a. A null hypothesis
   b. A nondirectional hypothesis
   c. A population
   d. A small level of sampling error
4. A high level of sampling error means that...
   a. The population may be too small
   b. Your sample may be too large
   c. You may not be able to generalize to your population
   d. Your hypotheses will not be supported
5. This type of hypothesis states that there is NO relationship between your variables:
   a. The null hypothesis
   b. The research hypothesis
   c. The population hypotheses
   d. The sample hypothesis
6. This type of hypothesis states that there IS a relationship between your variables:
   a. The null hypothesis
   b. The research hypothesis
   c. The population hypothesis
   d. The sample hypothesis
7. A one-tailed test would be used with the following type of hypothesis:
   a. A null hypothesis
   b. A research hypothesis
   c. A directional hypothesis
   d. A nondirectional hypothesis
8. A two-tailed test would be used with the following type of hypothesis:
   a. A null hypothesis
   b. A research hypothesis
   c. A directional hypothesis
   d. A nondirectional hypothesis
9. If you are unsure whether the null or research hypothesis is true, you must assume the following:
   a. The population was too small
   b. The sample was too small
   c. The research hypothesis is true

    d. The null hypothesis is true

10. Null hypotheses always refer to the following:
    a. The sample
    b. The population
    c. Sampling error
    d. Two-tailed tests

11. Research hypotheses always refer to the following:
    a. The sample
    b. The population
    c. Sampling error
    d. One-tailed tests

12. Null hypotheses are written using the following types of letters:
    a. Greek
    b. Roman
    c. Arabic
    d. Sanskrit

13. Research hypotheses are written using the following types of letters:
    a. Greek
    b. Roman
    c. Arabic
    d. Sanskrit

14. Which of the following is not a feature of good hypotheses?
    a. There should be no more than one null and research hypothesis in any study
    b. They should be brief and to the point
    c. They should be testable
    d. They should posit an expected relationship between variables

15. Which type of hypothesis is this?: There is no relationship between religiosity and drug use.
    a. Research hypothesis
    b. Null hypothesis
    c. Sample hypothesis
    d. Directional research hypothesis

16. Which type of hypothesis is this?: Individuals with a college degree will have higher incomes than those with no college degree.
    a. Null hypothesis
    b. Directional research hypothesis
    c. Nondirectional research hypothesis
    d. Sample hypothesis

17. Which type of hypothesis is this?: Group A will differ from Group B in regard to test scores.
    a. Null hypothesis
    b. Directional research hypothesis
    c. Nondirectional research hypothesis
    d. Sample hypothesis

18. What type of hypothesis is this an example of?: $H_1 : \overline{X}_A \neq \overline{X}_B$
    a. Null hypothesis

b. Directional research hypothesis
c. Nondirectional research hypothesis
d. Population hypothesis

19. What type of hypothesis is this an example of?: $H_1 : \overline{X}_A < \overline{X}_B$
    a. Null hypothesis
    b. Directional research hypothesis
    c. Nondirectional research hypothesis
    d. Population hypothesis

20. What type of hypothesis is this an example of?: $H_0 : \mu_A = \mu_B$
    a. Null hypothesis
    b. Directional research hypothesis
    c. Nondirectional research hypothesis
    d. Population hypothesis

Exercises
{Omitted}

Short-answer/essay questions
1. You are going to conduct a psychological study focusing on the relationship between watching violence on television and violent behavior. Generate a null hypothesis and two research hypotheses for this study (directional and nondirectional).
2. Now, write both the null and research hypotheses using the appropriate Greek or Roman letters.
3. Check the hypotheses you generated against the five features of a good hypotheses. Do your hypotheses fulfill all of the requirements?
4. Come up with written descriptions of the hypotheses given under question 18-20 in the *Multiple Choice* section.
5. What is wrong with this hypothesis?: Will the accelerated class score higher on a reading comprehension exam as compared with a regular class?
6. What is wrong with this hypothesis?: It is hypothesized that religious leaders during the Stone Age gave greater thought to the meaning of life as compared with others.

SPSS Questions
{Omitted}

Just for fun/Challenge yourself
1. Do some additional research on the difference between one-way and two-way statistical tests. How do they differ? Which of the two is more likely to be found significant, in general? Why is it justified to use a one-way statistical test with a directional hypothesis, but not with a nondirectional hypothesis?

Answer key

True/False questions
1. False. The opposite is true - a hypothesis is a more specific, testable version of a research question.
2. True.
3. True. These are some of the characteristics of good hypotheses.

Multiple choice questions
1. b. sample; population
2. a. A representative sample
3. d. A small level of sampling error
4. c. You may not be able to generalize to your population
5. a. The null hypothesis
6. b. The research hypothesis
7. c. A directional hypothesis
8. d. A nondirectional hypothesis
9. d. The null hypothesis is true
10. b. The population
11. a. The sample
12. a. Greek
13. b. Roman
14. a. There should be no more than one null and research hypothesis in any study
15. b. Null hypothesis
16. b. Directional research hypothesis
17. c. Nondirectional research hypothesis
18. c. Nondirectional research hypothesis
19. b. Directional research hypothesis
20. a. Null hypothesis

Exercises
{Omitted}

Short-answer/essay questions
1. An example of a null hypothesis could be: There will be no relationship between individuals who watch less than one hour of violent television per day and those that watch one hour or more of violent television per day in regard to the number of instances of violent behavior.

   An example of a directional research hypothesis could be: Individuals who watch one hour of violent television per day or more will exhibit a greater number of instances of violent behavior as compared with those who watch less than one hour of violent television per day.

An example of a nondirectional research hypothesis could be: There is a difference between individuals who watch less than one hour of violent television per day and those that watch one hour or more of violent television per day in regard to the number of instances of violent behavior.

2. Some examples (your subscripts do not have to match exactly):

   Null hypothesis: $H_0 : \mu_{<1\,hr} = \mu_{1+\,hr}$

   Nondirectional research hypothesis: $H_1 : \overline{X}_{<1\,hr} \neq \overline{X}_{1+\,hr}$

   Directional research hypothesis: $H_1 : \overline{X}_{<1\,hr} < \overline{X}_{1+\,hr}$

3. As a reminder, the five features are:
   - They are stated in declarative form, not as a question.
   - They posit an expected relationship between variables.
   - They reflect the theory or literature on which they are based.
   - There are brief and to the point.
   - They are testable hypotheses.

4.
   a. For question 18: $H_1 : \overline{X}_A \neq \overline{X}_B$
      i. The average score of individuals in Group A is different from the average score of individuals in Group B.
   b. For question 19: $H_1 : \overline{X}_A < \overline{X}_B$
      i. Individuals in Group B will have higher scores, on average, as compared with individuals in Group A.
   c. For question 20: $H_0 : \mu_A = \mu_B$
      i. There is no difference in the average score of individuals in Group A and the average score of individuals in Group B.

5. The problem with this hypothesis is that it is phrased as a question.

6. The problem with this hypothesis is that it is not testable (we don't have the data and can't collect it).

SPSS Questions
{Omitted}

Just for fun/Challenge yourself
   1. As mentioned in this chapter, one-way statistical tests are suited to directional hypotheses, while two-way tests are suited to non-directional hypotheses. In essence, a

two-way test examines both possibilities (i.e., that group 1 has a higher average than group 2, and the possibility that group 2 has a higher average than group 1). A one-way test only examines one possibility (i.e., that either group 1 has a higher average than group 2, or that group 2 has a higher average than group 1). Because the one-way test only examines one possibility, it is easier for this test, if indeed your research hypothesis is true, to be found significant and for your research hypothesis to be adequately supported. Because a two-way test needs to examine both "sides", or both possibilities, it is weaker in a sense, and it is more difficult for you to find a significant result. It is not justified to use a one-way test with a nondirectional hypothesis, as you are going into the analysis not knowing what you may find. Therefore, using a more powerful one-way test in situations where you don't initially start with a directional hypothesis is "cheating", in a sense.

Chapter 8: Are Your Curves Normal? Probability and Why It Counts

Chapter outline
- Why Probability?
- The Normal Curve (A.K.A. the Bell-Shaped Curve)
  - Hey, That's Not Normal!
  - More Normal Curve 101
- Our Favorite Standard Score: the Z-Score
  - What Z-Scores Represent
  - What Z-Scores Really Represent
  - Hypothesis Testing and Z-Scores: the First Step
- Using the Computer to Compute Z-Scores
- Summary
- Time to Practice

Learning objectives
- Review the importance of probability in statistics.
- Understand the normal curve and its relation to the field of statistics.
- Learn how to compute z-scores by hand and using SPSS.

Summary/key points
- The study of probability is the basis for the normal curve and the foundation for inferential statistics.
  - The normal curve provides a basis for understanding the probability associated with any possible outcome, such as attaining a certain score.
  - The study of probability is the basis for determining the degree of confidence we have in stating that a particular finding or outcome is true.
  - Probability allows us to determine the exact mathematical likelihood that a difference between groups, or an association between variables, is due to practice or treatment as compared with chance or error.
- The normal curve is the basis for probability and statistics.
  - The normal curve has no skew and is perfectly symmetrical about the mean.
  - The tails of the normal distribution are asymptotic, meaning they never touch the horizontal axis, which is equal to zero.
  - In the social and behavioral sciences, as well as in other fields, many things are normally distributed, including measures such as height and IQ.
  - Events that occur in the extremes of the normal curve have a very small probability, while more "average" values are much more common.
- The normal curve has many specific statistical features.
  - Over 99.5% of scores are within three standard deviations from the mean.
  - Approximately 68% of scores fall within one standard deviation from the mean.
  - Exactly 50% of scores fall on either side of the distribution (i.e., either side of the mean).

- The percentages or areas under the normal curve can be interpreted as probabilities.
- Standard scores are raw scores which have been adjusted for the particular mean and standard deviation of the distribution from which they are derived. They can be used to compare raw scores between different samples which have different distributions.
  - The most commonly used standard score is the z-score.
    - To calculate the z-score, you subtract the mean from the raw score, and divide this difference by the standard deviation.
    - Scores which fall below the mean will have negative z-scores, while scores which fall above the mean will have positive z-scores.
    - The score located one standard deviation above the mean is "1 z score" above the mean.
    - We can use z-scores and the normal distribution to determine the probability of some event occurring.
- A statistical test can be used to determine the probability of the differences between groups or relationships between variables in the data. After conducting the test, the calculated probability can be compared with a standard to see if the result is "significant".
  - The standard of 5%, which is equivalent to a probability of .05, is the most commonly used standard in statistics. This means we need to be at least 95% sure of the difference between groups or the relationship between variables in order to call it "significant".
    - This means a result is significant if we find a z-score which has less than a 5% chance of occurring.

Key terms
- Normal curve (Bell-shaped curve): A distribution of scores that is symmetrical about the mean and in which the median, mean, and mode are all equal. This type of distribution has asymptotic tails, which never reach zero.
- Asymptotic: The quality of the normal curve such that its tails never touch the horizontal axis (equal to zero).
- Standard scores: Raw scores that are adjusted for the mean and standard deviation of the distribution from which they come.
- Z-score: A specific type of standard score, in which the mean of scores is subtracted from the raw score, and then this difference is divided by the standard deviation.

True/False questions
1. The percentages of scores under sections of the normal curve depend on the mean and standard deviation of distribution.
2. You can compare z-scores across two or more different distributions.
3. Values for the area under the normal curve can be viewed/interpreted as probabilities.
4. When looking up z-scores using a z-table, it is very important to consider whether the z-score you are looking up is positive or negative.
5. A standard score is the same as a standardized score, like the score you received on the SATs.

Multiple choice questions
1. This percentage of the normal curve reflects all scores greater than zero:
   a. 10%
   b. 25%
   c. 50%
   d. 100%
2. The entire normal curve represents this percentage of scores:
   a. 25%
   b. 50%
   c. 99%
   d. 100%
3. In regard to the normal curve, this percentage of scores is within one standard deviation of the mean:
   a. 13.59%
   b. 2.15%
   c. 68.26%
   d. 99.99%
4. This percentage of scores is within two standard deviations of the mean:
   a. 0.13%
   b. 2.15%
   c. 68.26%
   d. 95.44%
5. If your set of scores has a mean of 57, what would the z-score be for a raw score of 57?
   a. -1
   b. 0
   c. 1
   d. 2
6. If a raw score is above the mean, the z-score must be:
   a. Negative
   b. Positive
   c. Equal to 0
   d. Impossible to compute
7. If a score is four standard deviations above the mean, this means that its z-score must be equal to:
   a. -4
   b. 4
   c. 0
   d. 1
   e. 4^4
8. Based on the normal curve, what percentage of scores have a z-score of 2 or greater?
   a. 7.16%
   b. 22.42%
   c. 2.28%
   d. 0.15%
9. Based on the normal curve, what percentage of scores have a z-score less than -0.5?
   a. 30.85%

b. 22.42%

c. 47.40%

d. 23.65%

10. Your last exam had a class average of 82 and a standard deviation of 8. What's the probability of any score being 90 or greater?

    a. 12.15%

    b. 17.31%

    c. 23.52%

    d. 15.87%

11. Using the same scenario, what's the probability of any score being a failing grade (65 or less)?

    a. 1.68%

    b. 2.42%

    c. 12.40%

    d. 7.14%

12. If your last exam had a class average of 72 and a standard deviation of 12, what would be the probability of a z-score being between 70 and 80?

    a. 31.61%

    b. 21.42%

    c. 17.67%

    d. 12.14%

13. This is the most common probability standard used by researchers when conducting analyses:

    a. 0.01

    b. 0.05

    c. 0.10

    d. 0.50

Exercises

1. In your set of scores, you have a mean of 5.8 and a standard deviation of 2.3. Calculate the z-scores for the following raw scores: 2.1, 5.7, 7.3, 12.4.

2. You are taking a standardized test, and you want to score in the top 5%. You know that the mean is 1000 and the standard deviation is 100. What is the minimum score you need in order to get into the top 5%?

3. You have a set of test scores with a mean of 27 and a standard deviation of 4.2. Calculate the raw scores for the following z-scores: -5.3, -2.1, 0, 1, 3.1.

Short-answer/essay questions

1. What are some examples of measures that you think may be normally distributed? In general, what does the distribution of a measure need to look like in order for it to be normally distributed?

1. Enter the following data into SPSS: 23, 33, 42, 47, 51, 61, 63, 67, 69, 71. Now, calculate the corresponding z-scores. What is your result?

Just for fun/Challenge yourself
1. First, look up the equation for the normal curve. Now, using this equation, calculate the area under the curve for z-score between 0 and 1.
2. You measure the height of 10 people, and come up with an average of 70 inches, and a standard deviation of 4 inches. Calculate the T scores for the following cases: 68 inches, 76 inches.

Answer key

True/False questions
1. False. The percentages of scores under the normal curve are constant in the sense that they're the same regardless of the mean and standard deviation of the distribution.
2. True. Because z-scores are standard scores, you're able to compare them between different distributions.
3. True. Values for the area under the normal curve can be represented as probabilities or percentages.
4. False. Because the normal curve is symmetrical, it doesn't matter whether the z-score you're looking up is positive or negative. The area under the curve from the mean to a certain z-score will be identical for the positive and negative version of that z-score.
5. False. A standard score is very different from a standardized score. Standardized scores come from a distribution with a predefined mean and standard deviation, like the SATs or GREs.

Multiple choice questions
1. c. 50%
2. d. 100%
3. c. 68.26%
4. d. 95.44%
5. b. 0
6. b. Positive
7. b. 4
8. c. 2.28%
9. a. 30.85%
10. d. 15.87%
11. a. 1.68%
12. a. 31.61%
13. b. 0.05

Exercises

1. The four z-scores:

$$z = \frac{X - \overline{X}}{s} = \frac{2.1 - 5.8}{2.3} = -1.61$$

$$z = \frac{X - \overline{X}}{s} = \frac{5.7 - 5.8}{2.3} = -0.04$$

$$z = \frac{X - \overline{X}}{s} = \frac{7.3 - 5.8}{2.3} = 0.65$$

$$z = \frac{X - \overline{X}}{s} = \frac{12.4 - 5.8}{2.3} = 2.87$$

2. To achieve a score in the top 5%, you would need to first find the z-score such that exactly 5% of scores lie between that z-score and the highest possible score (or "infinity"). This would mean that 95% of scores are below this score. As 95% of scores are below the z-score, this means that the z-score that we are looking for is well above the mean. We know that 50% scores lie below the mean, so you need to find a z-score such that the area between the mean and the z-score is 0.45 (this adds together to 95%). This corresponds to a z-score of approximately 1.645.

    Using the formula:

    $$X = z(s) + \overline{X} = 1.645(100) + 1000 = 1164.5$$

3. You have a set of test scores with a mean of 27 and a standard deviation of 4.2. Calculate the raw scores for the following z-scores: -5.3, -2.1, 0, 1, 3.1.

    $$X = z(s) + \overline{X} = -5.3(4.2) + 27 = 4.74$$

    $$X = z(s) + \overline{X} = -2.1(4.2) + 27 = 18.18$$

    $$X = z(s) + \overline{X} = 0(4.2) + 27 = 27$$

    $$X = z(s) + \overline{X} = 1(4.2) + 27 = 31.2$$

    $$X = z(s) + \overline{X} = 3.1(4.2) + 27 = 40.02$$

1. In this chapter, the examples of IQ and height were presented. Exam scores, as well as final class scores, could also be examples of normally distributed measures. While the mean would probably be around a C, you'd expect to see smaller numbers of students get very high grades, and also small numbers of students get very low ones. Health is another example. You'd expect most people to have typical health: pretty good, perhaps some minor problems but no major ones. However, there will also be smaller percentages of individuals who have very poor health or very excellent health. In essence, the distribution of any normally distributed measure needs to look like the "bell curve": you have a large hump representing typical cases, with the peak equal to the mean. However, you also have smaller numbers of individuals who have more extreme scores, both in the positive and negative.

SPSS Questions
1. The z-scores are presented in the final column in the following screenshot:

	var1	Zvar1
1	23.00	-1.81871
2	33.00	-1.20635
3	42.00	-.65522
4	47.00	-.34905
5	51.00	-.10410
6	61.00	.50826
7	63.00	.63073
8	67.00	.87567
9	69.00	.99815
10	71.00	1.12062

Just for fun/Challenge yourself
1. First, look up the equation for the normal curve. Now, using this equation, calculate the area under the curve for z-score between 0 and 1.

$$Area\ from\ z_x\ to\ z_y = \frac{1}{\sqrt{2\pi}} \int_x^y \ell^{\frac{-z^2}{2}}\, dz = \frac{1}{\sqrt{2\pi}} \int_0^1 \ell^{\frac{-z^2}{2}}\, dz = \frac{1}{\sqrt{2\pi}}(0.8556) = .3413$$

2. You measure the height of 10 people, and come up with an average of 70 inches, and a standard deviation of 4 inches. Calculate the T scores for the following cases: 68 inches, 76 inches.

First, we calculate the z-scores:

$$z = \frac{X - \overline{X}}{s} = \frac{68 - 70}{4} = -0.5$$

Then:

$$T = z \times 10 + 50 = -0.5 \times 10 + 50 = 45$$

$$T = z \times 10 + 50 = 1.5 \times 10 + 50 = 65$$

Chapter 9: Significantly Significant: What It Means for You and Me

<u>Chapter outline</u>
- The Concept of Significance
    - If Only We Were Perfect
    - The World's Most Important Table (for This Semester Only)
    - More about Table 9.1
    - Back to Type I Errors
- Significance Versus Meaningfulness
- An Introduction to Inferential Statistics
    - How Inference Works
    - How to Select What Test to Use
    - Here's How to Use the Chart
- An Introduction to Tests of Significance
    - How a Test of Significance Works: the Plan
    - Here's the Picture That's Worth a Thousand Words
- Be Even More Confident
- Summary
- Time to Practice

<u>Learning objectives</u>
- Understand the concept of statistical significance.
- Learn the difference between Type I errors and Type II errors.
- Understand the purpose of inferential statistics.
- Understand the distinction between statistical significance and meaningfulness.
- Learn the eight steps used to apply a statistical test to test any null hypothesis.
- Learn what confidence intervals are.

<u>Summary/key points</u>
- Statistical tests are based on probability: you are able to say with a certain level of certainty that there is a difference between groups or a relationship between variables, but you can't say this with 100% absolute certainty.
    - This introduces the possibility of making an error in judgment.
    - The level of chance or risk that you are willing to take is expressed as a significance level.
    - A significance level of .05 corresponds to a one in 20 chance that any differences or relationships found based on statistical tests that were conducted were not due to the hypothesized reason, but instead to chance.
        - Researchers should try as much as possible to reduce this likelihood by removing all competing reasons for any differences or relationships. However, this cannot be fully controlled as it is impossible to control for every possible factor.
    - There is always the possibility of error in statistics because the population itself is not directly tested. The sample is tested, and the results are inferred or

generalized to the larger population. There is always the possibility of error in this inferential process.

- The level of statistical significance is equal to the possibility of making a Type I error.
  - A Type I error occurs when you reject the null hypothesis when there is actually no difference between groups or relationships between variables.
  - Type I errors are represented by the Greek letter alpha, or α.
  - These significance levels are typically set between .01 and .05. .05 is the most common standard used.
    - A statistical test that is nearly significant can be called "marginally significant". For example, if the probability level is set at .05, and the significance of your result is, say, .052 or .055, it can be reported as a "marginally significant" result.
- A Type II error occurs when you accept a false null hypothesis.
  - This means that you conclude that there is no difference between groups or no relationship between variables when in fact there actually is.
  - Type II errors are represented by the Greek letter beta, or β.
  - Type II errors are not directly controlled, but are related to factors such as sample size. Type II errors decrease as the sample size increases.
- While Type I and Type II errors cover the scenarios in which errors are made, there are also two scenarios in which you make the correct judgment.
  - First, you can accept the null hypothesis when the null hypothesis is actually true. This means that you said that there is no difference between groups, or no relationship between variables, and are correct.
  - Secondly, you can reject the null hypothesis when the null hypothesis is actually false. This means that you said that there is a real difference between groups, or relationship between variables, and you are correct.
    - This is also called power, or $1-\beta$. This is simply equal to the value of the type II error subtracted from 1.
- There is an important difference between statistical significance and meaningfulness. It is possible to have a result that is statistically significant, but so small that it is not really meaningful.
- While descriptive statistics focuses on describing data (with tables, charts, etc.), inferential statistics are used to infer something about the population based on the sample's characteristics.
  - Inferential statistics uses a wide variety of statistical tests and analyses in order to test differences between groups or relationships between variables.
  - Tests of significance are used in inferential statistics. These tests of significance are based on the fact that each null hypothesis can be tested with a particular type of statistical test. Every calculated statistic has a special distribution associated with it. The calculated value is then compared to the distribution, and you can conclude whether the sample characteristics are different from what you would expect by chance.
- There are eight general steps that are used in order to apply a statistical test to any null hypothesis.
  1. Provide a statement of the null hypothesis.
  2. Set the level of risk associated with the null hypothesis (significance level).

3. Select the appropriate test statistic.
4. Compute the test statistic value (also known as the obtained value).
5. Determine the value (the critical value) needed for rejection of the null hypothesis using the appropriate table of critical values for that particular statistic.
6. Compare the obtained value with the critical value.
7. If the obtained value is more extreme than the critical value, the null hypothesis must be rejected.
8. If the obtained value does not exceed the critical value, the null hypothesis cannot be rejected.

- Confidence intervals represent the best estimate of the range of the population value (or population parameter) based on the sample value (or sample statistic).
    - A higher confidence interval (for example, a 99% confidence interval as compared with a 95% confidence interval) represents a greater degree of confidence, meaning that a wider range of values will be incorporated into the confidence interval.

Key terms

- Significance level or Statistical significance: The level of risk set by the researcher for rejecting a null hypothesis when it is true. In other words, it corresponds to the level of risk that there is actually no relationship between variables when the results of your analysis appear to tell you that there is.
- Type I error: The rejection, or the probability of rejection, of a null hypothesis when it is true.
- Type II error: Accepting, or the probability of accepting, a null hypothesis when it is false.
- Inferential statistics: A set of tools that are used to infer the results based on the sample to a population.
- Test statistic (a.k.a. Obtained value): The value that results from the use of a statistical test.
- Critical value: The value necessary for rejection (or nonacceptance) of the null hypothesis.
- Confidence interval: The best estimate of the range of a population value given the sample value.

True/False questions

1. A 99% confidence interval would have a larger range than a 95% confidence interval.
2. Using inferential statistics, it is commonly possible to say that you have 100% confidence in a result.

Multiple choice questions

1. A significance level of .05 corresponds to a _____ chance that any differences or relationships found based on the statistical test that was conducted were not due to the hypothesized reason, but instead to chance.

a. 1 in 10
b. 5 in 10
c. 1 in 5
d. 1 in 20

2. This relates to the rejection of the null hypothesis when it is actually false:
    a. Type I error
    b. Type II error
    c. Power
    d. Statistical significance

3. This relates to accepting the null hypothesis when it is actually true:
    a. Type I error
    b. Type II error
    c. Power
    d. A correct decision

4. This relates to the rejection of the null hypothesis when it is actually true:
    a. Type I error
    b. Type II error
    c. Power
    d. Statistical significance

5. This relates to accepting the null hypothesis when it is actually false:
    a. Type I error
    b. Type II error
    c. Power
    d. Statistical significance

6. This is calculated as subtracting the Type II error from 1:
    a. Type I error
    b. Type II error
    c. Power
    d. The significance level

7. Type I errors are represented as:
    a. α
    b. β
    c. $1-\beta$
    d. e

8. Type II errors are represented as:
    a. α
    b. β
    c. $1-\beta$
    d. e

9. You conduct a study in order to see whether there is a significant difference in IQ between two classes. The first class has an average IQ of 114.1, while the second class has an average IQ of 114.7. You conduct a statistical test which finds there to be a significant difference between these two groups at the .05 level of significance. In sum, these results are:
    a. Statistically significant only
    b. Meaningful only

c. Statistically significant and meaningful
   d. Neither statistically significant nor meaningful
10. When conducting a statistical test, you set the significance level at .05. After running the analysis, you find a significance level of .054. This result is:
   a. Statistically significant
   b. Marginally significant
   c. Meaningful only
   d. None of the above
11. In inferential statistics, you infer from a _____ to a _____.
   a. Larger population; smaller sample
   b. Smaller sample; larger population
   c. Smaller population; larger sample
   d. Larger sample; smaller population
12. Using z-scores, a 95% confidence interval would consist of the following range:
   a. ±1 z
   b. ±1.96 z
   c. ±2.05 z
   d. ±2.56 z
13. Using z-scores, a 99% confidence interval would consist of the following range:
   a. ±1 z
   b. ±1.96 z
   c. ±2.05 z
   d. ±2.56 z
14. If a class exam had a mean of 82 and a standard deviation of 12, what would be the 95% confidence interval?
   a. $12 \pm 2.56(82)$
   b. $82 \pm 2.56(12)$
   c. $12 \pm 1.96(82)$
   d. $82 \pm 1.96(12)$
15. Using the .05 level of significance, which of the following findings is statistically significant?
   a. Higher levels of crime are found in cities with greater population density ($p < .05$).
   b. Global temperatures have been found to be increasing steadily since 1900 ($p = .053$).
   c. Crime rates in the United States have been steadily decreasing since 1990 ($p = .06$).
   d. No gender differences in scores were found ($p = .12$).
16. You have the greatest chance of finding a significant result if the significance level is set at:
   a. 0.10
   b. 0.05
   c. 0.01
   d. 0.001
17. This is the value that results from the use of a statistical test.
   a. The critical value

b. The obtained value
c. Type I error
d. Type II error

18. This is the value necessary for rejection (or nonacceptance) of the null hypothesis.
    a. The critical value
    b. The obtained value
    c. Type I error
    d. Type II error

19. This is the best estimate of the range of a population value given the sample value.
    a. The critical value
    b. The obtained value
    c. Power
    d. Confidence interval

Exercises

1. Come up with a hypothesis in an area of study that you're interested in. Now, conduct a "mock" statistical test, writing out the eight steps used to apply a statistical test to your hypothesis.

Short-answer/essay questions

1. What's an example of a result that is statistically significant but not meaningful? Why is it not meaningful?

SPSS Questions
{Omitted}

Just for fun/Challenge yourself

1. Spend a few minutes reading about statistical power online or in a statistics book. Next, download G*Power, a free software program for power calculations, or find an online calculator which can calculate the power for correlation coefficients. Using a Pearson correlation (bivariate normal model), what is the sample size needed for a two-tailed test if the null correlation (ρ) is 0, the research hypothesis correlation (ρ) is 0.5, your level of significance is .05, and you want a power of 0.9?

Answer key

True/False questions

1. True. To have a higher level of confidence (i.e., 99% confidence instead of 95% confidence), you would need to incorporate a larger set of values into the range for the confidence interval. This means that a 99% confidence interval would have to have a larger range as compared with a 95% confidence interval.

2. False. Inferential statistics uses probability, which in this case means that you can never be completely certain of a result.

Multiple choice questions
1. d. 1 in 20
2. c. Power
3. d. A correct decision
4. a. Type I error
5. b. Type II error
6. c. Power
7. a. α
8. b. β
9. b. Meaningful only
10. b. Marginally significant
11. b. Smaller sample; larger population
12. b. ±1.96 z
13. d. ±2.56 z
14. d. $82 \pm 1.96(12)$
15. a. Higher levels of crime were found in cities with greater population density (p < .05).
16. a. 0.10
17. b. The obtained value
18. a. The critical value
19. d. Confidence interval

Exercises
1. As an example, let's say that I'm interested in crime rates, and want to study whether there is a significant difference in crime rates (per capita) between the United States and the continent of Europe. Your answer does not have to be as detailed as mine, and we will get more detailed and specific in the next few chapters. Here are the eight steps that we would use to test this:

    1. A statement of the null and research hypotheses:

        The null hypothesis: H_0: $\mu1 = \mu2$

        The research hypothesis: H_1: $\overline{X}_1 \neq \overline{X}_2$
    2. Set the level of significance associated with the null hypothesis: 0.05
    3. Select the appropriate test statistic: In order to test this, we would use the *t*-test for independent means, as we are testing the difference between two separate groups.
    4. In this step, the test statistic value (the obtained value) would be calculated. This goes beyond what we've covered so far, but we will fully complete this step in later chapters which focus on particular statistical tests. For sake of argument, say that our obtained value is 3.7.
    5. In this step, the critical value would be determined. Again, to continue with this example, say that our critical value is 2.021.

6. Now, the obtained value is compared with the critical value. As you can see, our obtained value is larger than our critical value.
7. As the obtained value is more extreme than the critical value, we can say that our null hypothesis cannot be accepted.
8. Because the obtained value was larger than the critical value, we would not accept the null hypothesis in step 8.

Short-answer/essay questions
1. A result that is statistically significant but not meaningful could be any difference between groups, or relationship between variables, which has a significance level below .05 (or whatever standard you're using), but in which there is a very small difference or relationship. For example, you would have a group difference that is significant but not meaningful if the class average on the first exam was 87.2, and the class average on the second exam was 88.1, and this had a significance level below .05. Also, you would have a significant but not meaningful relationship if the correlation between two variables had a significance level below .05, but the strength of the correlation was very weak.

The reason why these examples do not illustrate a meaningful difference between groups or a meaningful relationship between variables is because the group difference or strength of the relationship is extremely low.

SPSS Questions
{Omitted}

Just for fun/Challenge yourself
1. The minimum sample size needed in this example is 37.

Chapter outline
- Introduction to the One-Sample Z-Test
  - The Path to Wisdom and Knowledge
- Computing the Test Statistic
  - So How Do I Interpret z= 2.38, p<.05?
- Summary
- Time to Practice

Learning objectives
- Understand when it is appropriate to use the one-sample z-test.
- Learn how to compute the observed z value for a one sample z-test.
- Learn how to interpret the z value and understand what it means.
- Be able to go through the eight steps of testing a hypothesis when using the one sample z-test.

Summary/key points
- A one-sample z-test is used to compare the mean of a sample to the mean of a population.
  - This test is used when only one group is being tested.
  - The obtained value is determined by calculating the one-sample z-test.
  - After the z value is calculated, the critical value is obtained from a table of z-scores so that a comparison can be made.

Key terms
- One-sample z-test: A statistical test used for comparing a sample mean to a population mean.
- Standard error of the mean: An error term which is used as the denominator in the equation for the z value in a one-sample z-test. The standard error of the mean is the standard deviation of all possible means selected from the population.

True/False questions
1. A one-sample z-test can be used to compare the mean of two populations.
2. In order for a one sample z-test to be significant at the .05 level of significance, you need an obtained z value of at least 1.96 (or below -1.96).

Multiple choice questions
1. A one-sample z-test would be used in the following situation:
   a. Comparing two sample means
   b. Comparing two population means
   c. Comparing a sample mean with a population mean

      d. Comparing two sample means with a population mean
2. In a one-sample z-test, this many groups are being tested:
      a. 1
      b. 2
      c. 3
      d. Two or more
3. In the equation for a one-sample z-test, the denominator is known as:
      a. The sample mean
      b. The population mean
      c. The standard error of the mean
      d. The standard error of the population
4. This value represents the standard deviation of all the possible means selected from the population.
      a. The sample mean
      b. The population mean
      c. The standard error of the mean
      d. The standard error of the population
5. You conducted a one sample z-test, obtaining a value of 4.6 for the z value. What is your conclusion?
      a. You should reject the null hypothesis
      b. You should not reject the null hypothesis
      c. The result is too close to call
      d. None of the above

Exercises
1. You are a teacher at a gifted school and you feel that the newest class of students is even brighter than usual. The mean IQ at your school is 127, and the mean IQ of this new class is 134. In total, there are 32 students in this new class. Also, the standard deviation of the school's IQ is 8. Use the eight steps to test whether this new class of students is significantly more intelligent than the school overall.
2. Interpret the following result: $z = 3.49$, $p < .05$

Short-answer/essay questions
1. Come up with two examples in which a one-sample z-test would be appropriate.

SPSS Questions
{Omitted}

Just for fun/Challenge yourself
1. A one-sample z-test was conducted in which the sample mean was 76, the population mean was 82, the population standard deviation was 2, and the calculated z value was -15. What was the sample size?

True/False questions
1. False. The one-sample z-test is used to compare the mean of a sample with the mean of a population, not to compare the mean of two populations.
2. True. At the .05 level of significance, a two-tailed test has a critical value of 1.96 for the z value.

Multiple choice questions
1. c. Comparing a sample mean with a population mean
2. a. 1
3. c. The standard error of the mean
4. c. The standard error of the mean
5. a. You should reject the null hypothesis

Exercises
1. The eight steps used in order to test this hypothesis are presented here:
    1. The null hypothesis: $H_0 : \overline{X} = \mu$

        The alternative hypothesis: $H_1 : \overline{X} > \mu$
    2. The level of significance: 0.05
    3. The appropriate test statistic: The one-sample z-test
    4. Computation of the test statistic value

    $$SEM = \frac{\sigma}{\sqrt{n}} = \frac{8}{\sqrt{32}} = 1.41$$

    $$z = \frac{\overline{X} - \mu}{SEM} = \frac{134 - 127}{1.41} = 4.96$$

    5. As this is a one-tailed test, the value needed for rejection of the null hypothesis is ±1.66. This represents the point at which only 5% of scores are higher than this value, corresponding to our significance level of .05. If we had been conducting a two-tailed test, the critical value would be ±1.96.
    6. Comparing the obtained value with the critical value, we see that the obtained value is higher than the critical value.

    7 & 8. As our obtained value is greater than the critical value, we can reject the null hypothesis which suggests no difference between the sample and population mean. Our results clearly show that this new class is significantly brighter than the school overall.

2. First, the "z" represents the test statistic that was used. The value of 3.49 represents the obtained z value that was calculated as part of conducting the one-sample z-test. Finally, p<.05 indicates that we have at least a 95% level of certainty that these two groups (the sample and the population) do actually differ in regard to their mean values.

Short-answer/essay questions

1. These two examples could be any situation in which you are comparing a sample mean to a population mean. For example, a one-sample z-test would be appropriate if you are comparing reading test scores in one school with scores of the entire nation. Another example could be testing whether the crime rate in a certain state or neighborhood is significantly different from the national crime rate.

SPSS Questions
{Omitted}

Just for fun/Challenge yourself

1. We can solve this using the equation for the one-sample z-test:

$$z = \frac{\overline{X} - \mu}{\sigma / \sqrt{n}} \Rightarrow -15 = \frac{76 - 82}{2 / \sqrt{n}} \Rightarrow -15 = \frac{-6}{2 / \sqrt{n}} \Rightarrow -15 = -6\left(\frac{\sqrt{n}}{2}\right) \Rightarrow -15 = -3\sqrt{n} \Rightarrow$$

$$5 = \sqrt{n} \Rightarrow n = 25$$

Chapter 11: t(ea) for Two: Test between the Means of Different Groups

Chapter outline
- Introduction to the t-Test for Independent Samples
  - The Path to Wisdom and Knowledge
- Computing the Test Statistic
  - So How Do I Interpret $t(58) = -.14$, $p > .05$?
- Special Effects: Are Those Differences for Real?
  - Computing and Understanding the Effect Size
  - A Very Cool Effect Size Calculator
- Using the Computer to Perform a t-Test
  - What the SPSS Output Means
- Summary
- Time to Practice

Learning objectives
- Understand when it is appropriate to use the t-test for independent means.
- Learn how to calculate the observed t value by hand and using SPSS.
- Learn how to interpret the results of a t-test.
- Understand the difference between a significant and meaningful result and how this relates to the effect size.

Summary/key points
- The t-test for independent means is used when you are looking at the difference in average scores of one or more variables between two groups that are independent of one another (i.e., are not related in any way).
  - This test is used when each group is tested only once.
  - There must be only two groups in total.
  - The corresponding test statistic is the t-test for independent means.
- After the t-test for independent means is conducted, the obtained value is compared with the critical value in order to see whether you have statistical significance.
- There's an important difference between a significant result and a meaningful result.
- Effect size is used to determine the size of an effect.
  - A small effect size ranges from 0 to .20
  - A medium effect size ranges from .20 to .50
  - A large effect size is any value above .50
  - A larger effect size represents a greater difference between the two groups.

Key terms
- Homogeneity of variance assumption: An assumption underlying the t-test which states that the amount of variability in both groups is equal.

- Degrees of freedom: A value that approximates the sample size and is a component of many statistical tests.
- Effect size: A measure of how different groups are from one another (i.e., a measure of the magnitude of the effect).
- Pooled standard deviation: Part of the formula for the effect size which is similar to an average of the standard deviations from both groups.

True/False questions
1. The following observed value: $t_{(24)} = 2.35$ is significant at the .05 level (two-tailed).
2. The t-test for independent samples should be used when participants are tested multiple times.
3. The sign of the observed t value (i.e., whether it is positive or negative) is a crucial element in the conducting of the t-test for independent samples.

Multiple choice questions
1. Which of the following is significant at the .05 level (two-tailed)?
    a. $t_{(32)} = 2.01$
    b. $t_{(212)} = 1.99$
    c. $t_{(6)} = 2.30$
    d. $t_{(2)} = 4.10$
2. Which of the following is significant at the .01 level (one-tailed)?
    a. $t_{(1)} = 28.90$
    b. $t_{(16)} = 2.42$
    c. $t_{(70)} = 2.45$
    d. $t_{(80)} = 2.37$
3. The t-test for independent samples should be used in the following scenario:
    a. You are comparing more than two groups that are related
    b. You are comparing exactly two groups that are related
    c. You are comparing exactly two groups that are unrelated
    d. You are comparing more than two groups that are unrelated
4. The assumption that the t-test for independent samples makes regarding the amount of variability in each of the two groups is called:
    a. The homogeneity of variance assumption
    b. The equality of variance assumption
    c. The assumption of variance equivalence
    d. The variability equality assumption
5. The value used in the equation for the t-test for independent means that approximates the sample size is known as:
    a. The homogeneity of variances
    b. The sample size
    c. The degrees of freedom
    d. The standard deviation

6. When looking up a critical t value in a t table, if your observed t value lies between two critical values in the table, to be conservative, you would select, for the degrees of freedom:
    a. The smaller value
    b. The larger value
    c. The smallest value in the table
    d. The largest value in the table
7. After conducting a t-test for independent samples, you arrived at the following: $t_{(47)} = 3.41, p < .05$. The degrees of freedom is indicated by:
    a. 47
    b. 3.41
    c. $< .05$
    d. p
    e. t
8. After conducting a t-test for independent samples, you arrived at the following: $t_{(47)} = 3.41, p < .05$. The t value is indicated by:
    a. 47
    b. 3.41
    c. $< .05$
    d. p
    e. t
9. After conducting a t-test for independent samples, you arrived at the following: $t_{(47)} = 3.41, p < .05$. The probability is indicated by:
    a. 47
    b. 3.41
    c. $< .05$
    d. t
10. After conducting a t-test for independent samples, you arrived at the following: $t_{(47)} = 3.41, p < .05$. The test statistic that was used is indicated by:
    a. 47
    b. 3.41
    c. $< .05$
    d. p
    e. t
11. An effect size of .25 would be considered:
    a. Small
    b. Medium
    c. Large
12. An effect size of .17 would be considered:
    a. Small
    b. Medium
    c. Large
13. An effect size of .55 would be considered:
    a. Small
    b. Medium
    c. Large

14. If there is no difference between the distributions of scores in two groups, your effect size will be equal to:
    a. 0
    b. 0.1
    c. 0.5
    d. 1

Exercises
1. You are interested in exploring whether your afternoon class has significantly different test scores than your morning class. You have 12 students in each class, and you decide to conduct a t-test for independent samples on the last exam you gave. This is your data:

Class 1 Exam Scores	*Class 2 Exam Scores*
87	86
98	73
75	79
88	56
76	72
85	70
92	87
56	59
89	64
85	77
84	74
92	72

Use the eight steps to test the null hypothesis that there is no difference between your two classes.

2. Assuming that the standard deviations between the two groups are equal to one another, calculate the effect size if your two groups have means of 47.7 and 58.2, and you have a standard deviation of 4.3. Is this effect size small, medium, or large?
3. Using the following online calculator: http://www.uccs.edu/~faculty/lbecker/ calculate the effect size using the data from the previous question. Do your results match?
4. Interpret the following result: $t_{(21)} = 28.90, p < .05$

Short-answer/essay questions
{Omitted}

1. Input the data under the "Exercises" section, question 1, into SPSS. Now, use SPSS to conduct a t-test for independent samples. How would you interpret the results? Do your results match those calculated by hand?

Just for fun/Challenge yourself
1. You study two apple orchards to see if one produces significantly more fruit than the other. The first orchard produces an average of 14.2 tons of apples per year, while the second produces 17.3 tons per year, on average. The standard deviation of the amount of apples produced per year is 4.2 tons for the first orchard, and 2.3 tons for the second orchard. Calculate the effect size using the equation which utilizes the pooled standard deviation.

Answer key

True/False questions
1. True.
2. False. This test should only be used when participants are tested only once.
3. False. The sign of the observed t value is not important, as the t-test for independent samples is nondirectional.

Multiple choice questions
1. b. $t_{(212)} = 1.99$
2. c. $t_{(70)} = 2.45$
3. c. You are comparing exactly two groups that are unrelated
4. a. The homogeneity of variance assumption
5. c. The degrees of freedom
6. a. The smaller value
7. a. 47
8. b. 3.41
9. c. $< .05$
10. e. t
11. b. Medium
12. a. Small
13. c. Large
14. a. 0

Exercises
1. The eight steps to test this hypothesis would consist of the following:

    1. A statement of the null and research hypotheses:
        The null hypothesis: $H_0: \mu_1 = \mu_1$

The research hypothesis: $H_1 : \overline{X}_1 \neq \overline{X}_2$

2. Set the level of risk associated with the null hypothesis: .05.
3. Select the appropriate test statistic: the t-test for independent means.
4. Compute the test statistic value (obtained value):

$$t = \frac{\overline{X}_1 - \overline{X}_2}{\sqrt{\left[\dfrac{(n_1-1)s_1^2 + (n_2-1)s_2^2}{n_1+n_2-2}\right]\left[\dfrac{n_1+n_2}{n_1 n_2}\right]}}$$

$$t = \frac{83.92 - 72.42}{\sqrt{\left[\dfrac{(12-1)10.89^2 + (12-1)9.49^2}{12+12-2}\right]\left[\dfrac{12+12}{12\times12}\right]}} = \frac{11.50}{\sqrt{\dfrac{1304.92+990.92}{22}\left[\dfrac{24}{144}\right]}} = 2.76$$

5. Determine the value needed for rejection of the null hypothesis using the appropriate table of critical values. With a degrees of freedom of 22, a two-tailed test using the .05 level of significance has a critical value of 2.074.
6. Compare the obtained value with the critical value: In this case, the obtained value is higher than the critical value.
7. & 8. Decision Time: As the obtained value is greater than the critical value, we choose to reject the null hypothesis that there is no difference between classes.

2. The effect size would be calculated using the following equation:

$$ES = \frac{\overline{X}_1 - \overline{X}_2}{SD} = \frac{47.7 - 58.2}{4.3} = -2.44$$

While this effect size was calculated to be negative, we can treat all effect sizes to be positive. The effect size of 2.44 would be considered large.

3. Using this calculator, we would use 4.3 for the standard deviation of both samples. The calculated effect size (Cohen's *d*) is identical to what we had calculated, -2.44.

4. First, *t* represents the test statistic that was used. 21 is the degrees of freedom, and 28.90 is the obtained value for the test statistic. Finally, $p < .05$ indicates that the probability is less than 5% that on any one test of the null hypothesis, the two groups do not differ.

Short-answer/essay questions
{Omitted}

1. The following is the output from SPSS for this t-test for independent samples:

Group Statistics

	Class	N	Mean	Std. Deviation	Std. Error Mean
Exam	1.00	12	83.9167	10.89168	3.14416
	2.00	12	72.4167	9.49122	2.73988

Independent Samples Test

		Levene's Test for Equality of Variances		t-test for Equality of Means				
		F	Sig.	t	df	Sig. (2-tailed)	Mean Difference	Std. Error Difference
Exam	Equal variances assumed	.037	.850	2.757	22	.011	11.50000	4.17045
	Equal variances not assumed			2.757	21.596	.012	11.50000	4.17045

These results do match those that were calculated by hand. This result was found to be statistically significant at the .05 level, meaning that the null hypothesis which states that there is no difference between the two groups of respondents should be rejected.

Just for fun/Challenge yourself

1. The effect size using the pooled standard deviation would be calculated using the following equation:

$$ES = \frac{\overline{X}_1 - \overline{X}_2}{\sqrt{\dfrac{\sigma_1^2 + \sigma_2^2}{2}}} = \frac{14.2 - 17.3}{\sqrt{\dfrac{4.2^2 + 2.3^2}{2}}} = -.92$$

Chapter 12: t(ea) for Two (Again): Tests between the Means of Related Groups

Chapter outline
- Introduction to the t-Test for Dependent Samples
  - The Path to Wisdom and Knowledge
- Computing the Test Statistic
- So How Do I Interpret $t_{(24)} = 2.45$, $p < .05$?
- Using the Computer to Perform a t-Test
  - What the SPSS Output Means
- Summary
- Time to Practice

Learning objectives
- Understand the purpose of the t-test for dependent means and when it should be used.
- Learn how to compute the observed t value for this test by hand and using SPSS.
- Learn how to interpret the t value and understand what it means.

Summary/key points
- The t-test for dependent means is used in order to determine whether there is a significant difference in the scores of a group of respondents who are tested at two points in time.
  - This t-test is also known as the t-test for paired samples or the t-test for correlated samples.

Key terms
- t-Test for Dependent Means: A test of the difference in means in a group of respondents that were tested at two points in time.

True/False questions
1. The following observed value: $t_{(37)} = 5.62$ is significant at the .05 level (two-tailed).
2. The t-test for dependent means should be used when participants are tested two or more times.

Multiple choice questions
1. The t-test for dependent means should be used in the following scenario:
   a. You are comparing more than two groups that are related
   b. You are comparing exactly two groups that are related
   c. You are comparing exactly two groups that are unrelated
   d. You are comparing more than two groups that are unrelated
2. If you are running a t-test for dependent means on a group of 25 individuals, your degrees of freedom will be:
   a. 25

    b. 26

    c. 24

    d. 12.5

3. If you are hypothesizing that posttest scores will be lower than pretest scores, you should use a:

    a. One-tailed test

    b. Two-tailed test

    c. t-Test for independent means

    d. Descriptive statistics

4. After conducting a t-test for dependent means, you arrived at the following: $t_{(22)} = 12.41$, $p < .05$. The degrees of freedom is indicated by:

    a. t

    b. $p < .05$

    c. 22

    d. 12.41

5. After conducting a t-test for dependent means, you arrived at the following: $t_{(22)} = 12.41$, $p < .05$. The test statistic is indicated by:

    a. t

    b. $p < .05$

    c. 22

    d. 12.41

6. After conducting a t-test for dependent means, you arrived at the following: $t_{(22)} = 12.41$, $p < .05$. The obtained value is indicated by:

    a. t

    b. $p < .05$

    c. 22

    d. 12.41

7. After conducting a t-test for dependent means, you arrived at the following: $t_{(22)} = 12.41$, $p < .05$. The probability is indicated by:

    a. t

    b. $p < .05$

    c. 22

    d. 12.41

Exercises

1. Using the following data, conduct the eight steps of hypothesis testing in order to see whether there is a difference between the income of these individuals before and after going back to school to get a masters degree.

Before ($1000)	After ($1000)
14	22
24	24
35	44
57	59
35	30
34	67
88	95
57	65

Short-answer/essay questions

1. After conducting a t-test for dependent means, you found the following result: $t_{(12)} = 0.12$, $p > .05$. Interpret this result.

SPSS Questions

1. Input the data in the "Exercises" section, question 1, into SPSS and run a t-test for dependent means. How would you interpret the results? Do your results match those calculated by hand?

Just for fun/Challenge yourself

{Omitted}

Answer key

True/False questions

1. True.
2. False. This test should only be used when participants are tested exactly twice.

Multiple choice questions

1. b. You are comparing exactly two groups that are related
2. c. 24
3. a. One-tailed test
4. c. 22
5. a. t
6. d. 12.41
7. b. $p < .05$

Exercises
1. The eight steps to test this hypothesis would consist of the following:

    1. A statement of the null and research hypotheses:
        The null hypothesis: H_0 : $\mu_{pretest} = \mu_{posttest}$

        The research hypothesis: H_1 : $\overline{X}_{pretest} \neq \overline{X}_{posttest}$
    2. Set the level of risk associated with the null hypothesis: .05.
    3. Select the appropriate test statistic: the t-test for dependent means.
    4. Compute the test statistic value (obtained value):

    $$t = \frac{\sum D}{\sqrt{\frac{n\sum D^2 - (\sum D)^2}{n-1}}} = \frac{62}{\sqrt{\frac{8 \times 1376 - 3844}{7}}} \quad 1.938$$

    5. Determine the value needed for rejection of the null hypothesis using the appropriate table of critical values. With a degrees of freedom of 7, a two-tailed test using the .05 level of significance has a critical value of 2.365.
    6. Compare the obtained value with the critical value: In this case, the obtained value is lower than the critical value.
    7. & 8. Decision Time: As the obtained value is lower than the critical value, we are not able to reject the null hypothesis that there is no difference between "before" and "after" values for salary.

Short-answer/essay questions
1. First, you can see that the test statistic used here was the t-test for dependent means. The degrees of freedom was 12, and the obtained t value was found to be 0.12. Finally, this result had a probability level above .05, meaning that no significant differences were found between pretest and posttest scores.

SPSS Questions
1. The following consists of the SPSS output for this test:

Paired Samples Statistics

		Mean	N	Std. Deviation	Std. Error Mean
Pair 1	Before	43.0000	8	23.38498	8.26784
	After	50.7500	8	25.38700	8.97566

Paired Samples Correlations

		N	Correlation	Sig.
Pair 1	Before & After	8	.896	.003

Paired Samples Test

		Paired Differences					t	df	Sig. (2-tailed)
					95% Confidence Interval of the Difference				
		Mean	Std. Deviation	Std. Error Mean	Lower	Upper			
Pair 1	Before - After	-7.75000	11.31055	3.99888	-17.20586	1.70586	-1.938	7	.094

In this test, the two-tailed significance level was found to be .094; as this value is not below .05, we're not able to reject the null hypothesis that there is no difference between "before" and "after" scores. The calculated result for the t value was identical to the result calculated by hand (remember, we can ignore the negative sign if the obtained t value is found to be negative).

Just for fun/Challenge yourself
{Omitted}

Chapter 13: Two Groups Too Many? Try Analysis of Variance

Chapter outline
- Introduction to Analysis of Variance
  - The Path to Wisdom and Knowledge
  - Different Flavors of ANOVA
- Computing the F Test Statistic
  - So How Do I Interpret $F_{(2, 27)} = 8.80$, $p < .05$?
- Using the Computer to Compute the F Ratio
  - What the SPSS Output Means
- Summary
- Time to Practice

Learning objectives
- Understand what an analysis of variance is and when it should be used.
- Understand the difference between the t-test and ANOVA.
- Learn how to compute and interpret the F statistic, both by hand and using SPSS.

Summary/key points
- Analysis of variance is used to test whether there is a significant difference in the mean of some dependent variable on the basis of group membership. Unlike the t-test, ANOVA can be used to test the difference between two groups as well as more than two groups of respondents.
  - The corresponding test statistic for ANOVA is the F test.
  - The type of ANOVA covered in this chapter (the simple analysis of variance) is used for participants who are tested only once.
- In essence, in an ANOVA, the variance due to differences in scores is separated into variance that's due to differences between individuals within groups and variance due to differences between groups. Then, these two types of variance are compared.
  - There are several types of ANOVA.
    - The simple analysis of variance, or one-way analysis of variance, includes only one factor or treatment variable in the analysis.
    - A factorial design includes more than one treatment factor.
  - ANOVA is an omnibus test, meaning that it tests overall differences between groups, and does not tell you which groups are higher or lower than others.
    - Post hoc comparisons can be used in order to determine whether there are significant differences between specific groups.

Key terms
- Analysis of Variance: A test for the difference between two or more means.
- Simple Analysis of Variance (a.k.a. One-Way Analysis of Variance): A type of ANOVA in which there is one factor or treatment variable (such as group membership) that is being explored.

- Factorial Design: A more complex type of ANOVA in which there is more than one treatment factor being explored.
- Post Hoc Comparisons: In relation to ANOVA, tests that are done in addition to ANOVA in order to look at specific group comparisons.

True/False questions
1. The F statistic obtained from running an analysis of variance will tell you which groups have significantly higher, or significantly lower, scores as compared with every other group.
2. All F tests are nondirectional.

Multiple choice questions
1. ANOVA is appropriate for the following situation:
    a. Two groups of participants are tested only once
    b. Two groups of participants are tested twice
    c. Three groups of participants are tested only once
    d. Four groups of participants are tested twice
    e. Both A and C
2. The corresponding test statistic for the ANOVA is:
    a. The p statistic
    b. The t statistic
    c. The F statistic
    d. The r statistic
3. This type of ANOVA is used when there is only one treatment factor:
    a. The simple analysis of variance
    b. A factorial design
    c. Post hoc comparisons
    d. Independent-samples t-test
4. This type of ANOVA is used when there are two or more treatment factors:
    a. The simple analysis of variance
    b. A factorial design
    c. Post hoc comparisons
    d. Independent-samples t-test
5. This type of test is used in order to look at specific group comparisons:
    a. The simple analysis of variance
    b. A factorial design
    c. Post hoc comparisons
    d. Independent-samples t-test
6. If you ran a factorial ANOVA using gender and social class, which is categorized as low, medium, and high, your factorial design would be the following:
    a. 2 x 2
    b. 3 x 2
    c. 1 x 1
    d. 1 x 3

Exercises

1. If you have a MS between of 2.4, and a MS within 0.3, what would your calculated F statistic be?

2. You are interested in testing whether three groups of respondents - office workers, students, and rock 'n roll musicians - significantly differ in their self-rated happiness. The happiness score is calculated on a scale of zero to 100, with 100 being the highest possible happiness score. Using the following data, conduct the eight steps of hypothesis testing.

Office Workers	Students	Rock & Roll Musicians
23	47	88
43	77	98
56	84	78
89	55	76
45	67	82
55	76	95
23	45	79
33	67	85
27	87	94
26	66	87

3. Using the results from the previous section, construct an F table (an example is presented on page 230 of the text).

Short-answer/essay questions

1. What is the critical F statistic value if your total sample size is 50 and you are comparing three groups of respondents (at the .05 level of significance)?

2. What is the critical F statistic value at the .05 level of significance for the following: $F_{(4, 70)}$?

3. How would you interpret $F_{(2, 30)} = 32.60$, $p < .05$?

SPSS Questions

1. Run an analysis of variance using the data in the "Exercises" section, question 2 (additionally, run the Bonferroni post hoc comparison). Do your results match those calculated by hand? How would you interpret these results?

Just for fun/Challenge yourself

1. If you are only comparing two groups of respondents, and the t value was found to be 2.30, what would be F statistic be?

2. If someone performs multiple t-tests, and their initial type I error rate is .05, and 8 comparisons were made, what would their actual type I error rate be?

Answer key

True/False questions
1. False. Post hoc comparisons are necessary for this – the F statistic is nondirectional.
2. True.

Multiple choice questions
1. e. Both A and C
2. c. The F statistic
3. a. The simple analysis of variance
4. b. A factorial design
5. c. Post hoc comparisons
6. b. 3 x 2

Exercises
1. This would be calculated in the following way:

$$F = \frac{MS_{between}}{MS_{within}} = \frac{2.4}{0.3} = 8.0$$

2. The eight steps of hypothesis testing are presented here:

1. State the null and research hypotheses:
   H_0: $\mu_1 = \mu_2 = \mu_3$
   H_1: $\overline{X}_1 \neq \overline{X}_2 \neq \overline{X}_3$

2. Set the level of significance: 0.05
3. Select the appropriate test statistic: A simple ANOVA
4. Compute the test statistic value:

	Office Workers	Students	Musicians
n	10	10	10
ΣX	420	671	862
$\Sigma(X^2)$	21508	46923	74828
$(\Sigma X)^2/n$	17640.0	45024.1	74304.4

$\Sigma\Sigma X = 1953$
$(\Sigma\Sigma X)^2/N = 127140.3$
$\Sigma\Sigma(X^2) = 143259$
$\Sigma(\Sigma X)^2/n = 136968.5$

Between SS = $\Sigma(\Sigma X)^2/n - (\Sigma\Sigma X)^2/N = 136968.5 - 127140.3 = 9828.2$
Within SS = $\Sigma\Sigma(X^2) - \Sigma(\Sigma X)^2/n = 143259 - 136968.5 = 6290.5$

MS Between = Between SS / (k-1) = 9828.2 / 2 = 4914.1
MS Within = Within SS / (N – k) = 6290.5 / (30-3) = 232.98

F = MS Between / MS Within = 4914.1 / 232.98 = 21.09223

5. Determine the value needed to reject the null hypothesis: Critical $F_{(2, 27)} = 3.36$
6. Compare the obtained value with the critical value: The obtained value, 21.09, is larger than the critical value of 3.36.
7. and 8. Decision: As the obtained value is greater than the critical value, we would reject the null hypothesis that there is no difference between these groups.

3. This table is shown here:

Source	Sum of Squares	df	Mean Sum of Squares	F
Between groups	9828.2	2	4914.1	21.09
Within groups	6290.5	27	232.98	
Total	16118.7	29		

Short-answer/essay questions
1. The critical F statistic in this case would be 3.21. This result is obtained by being more conservative and looking at the value which corresponds to a denominator degrees of freedom of 45.
2. The critical F statistic in this case would be 2.51.
3. First, the *F* represents the test statistic that was used. 2 and 30 represent the degrees of freedom for the between-group and within-group estimates, respectively. The value of 32.60 represents the obtained value which was arrived at by using the formula for the *F* statistic. Finally, $p<.05$ indicates that the probability is less than 5% that the average scores between groups differ due to chance as opposed to the effect of the treatment or group membership. This also indicates that the research hypothesis should be preferred over the null hypothesis, as there is a significant difference.

SPSS Questions
1. Run an analysis of variance using the data in the "Exercises" section, question 2 (additionally, run the Bonferroni post hoc comparison). Do your results match those calculated by hand? How would you interpret these results? The SPSS output is shown here:

Oneway

ANOVA

Score

	Sum of Squares	df	Mean Square	F	Sig.
Between Groups	9828.200	2	4914.100	21.092	.000
Within Groups	6290.500	27	232.981		
Total	16118.700	29			

Post Hoc Tests

Multiple Comparisons

Score

Bonferroni

(I) Group	(J) Group	Mean Difference (I-J)	Std. Error	Sig.	95% Confidence Interval	
					Lower Bound	Upper Bound
1	2	-25.100*	6.826	.003	-42.52	-7.68
	3	-44.200*	6.826	.000	-61.62	-26.78
2	1	25.100*	6.826	.003	7.68	42.52
	3	-19.100*	6.826	.028	-36.52	-1.68
3	1	44.200*	6.826	.000	26.78	61.62
	2	19.100*	6.826	.028	1.68	36.52

*. The mean difference is significant at the 0.05 level.

These results, in regard to the one-way ANOVA, do match those calculated by hand. First, the *F* test was found to be statistically significant, indicating that the null hypothesis should be rejected in favor of the research hypothesis, indicating that there is a significant difference between groups. Additionally, the Bonferroni post hoc comparison finds a significant difference between all three groups of respondents. Focusing on the final row, which compares group 3 (musicians) against groups 1 (office workers) and 2 (students), we can see that, looking at the mean difference and significance columns, that musicians are significantly happier than both students and offers workers (no surprise). Additionally, the only other comparison, which was between groups 1 and 2, is shown in the first row of results. Here, we can see that office workers are significantly less happy as compared with students (again, no surprise here).

Just for fun/Challenge yourself

1. In order to obtain the F statistic in this case, we simply need to square the t value: this gives us a calculated F statistic of 5.29.

2. If someone performs multiple t-tests, and their initial type I error rate is .05, and 8 comparisons were made, what would their actual type I error rate be? This can be calculated by the using the following equation:

$$\textit{True Type I Error} = 1 - (1 - \alpha)^k = 1 - (1 - .05)^8 = 0.34$$

Chapter 14: Two Too Many Factors: Factorial Analysis of Variance

Learning objectives
- Learn when it is appropriate to use the factorial analysis of variance.
- Understand the distinction between main effects and interaction effects and what they indicate.
- Learn how to use SPSS to conduct a factorial analysis of variance.

Summary/key points
- The factorial analysis of variance, or two-way analysis of variance, is used when you have more than one independent, or treatment variable.
  - This type of ANOVA can test the significance of the main effects of each independent variable, as well as the significance of the interaction effect between independent variables.
  - This type of ANOVA is used when participants are tested only once.
  - The test statistic used is the factorial analysis of variance.

Key terms
- Factorial analysis of variance (a.k.a. Two-way analysis of variance): the type of ANOVA that is used when there is more than one independent variable or factor.
- Main effect: In analysis of variance, when a factor or independent variable has a significant effect on the outcome variable.
- Source table: A listing of sources of variance in an analysis of variance summary table.
- Interaction effect: A phenomenon where the effect of one independent variable on the dependent variable differs based on the level of a second independent variable.

True/False questions
1. A factorial analysis of variance can be used only in the case where you have two independent, or treatment variables.
2. Interaction effects are always significant when all main effects are significant.

1. A factorial analysis of variance should be used in the following situation:
    a. You have two independent variables, and participants are tested more than once
    b. You have one independent variable, and participants are tested more than once
    c. You have two independent variables, and participants are tested only once
    d. You have three independent variables, and participants are tested more than once
1. In a factorial analysis of variance...
    a. The number of main effects will be equal to the number of independent variables
    b. The number of main effects will be equal to the number of independent variables plus the number of interaction effects
    c. The number of main effects will be equal to the number of interaction effects
    d. The number of main effects will be equal to the number of independent variables minus the number of interaction effects
1. What does the following constitute: "The effect of being upper class, middle class, or lower class is different for males and females"
    a. An interaction effect
    b. A main effect
    c. Could be either an interaction effect or a main effect
    d. None of the above
2. When plotted on a graph, a significant interaction effect is indicated by the following:
    a. Parallel lines
    b. Lines that cross/are not parallel
    c. Either a. or b. could be true
    d. None of the above

Exercises
1. Draw an example of a graph which illustrates a strong interaction effect. Now, draw a graph that illustrates no interaction effect at all.

Short-answer/essay questions
1. In what situations would a factorial ANOVA be preferred over the one-way ANOVA and why?

SPSS Questions
1. Using the following data, use the eight steps of hypothesis testing in order to determine the main effects of group membership and the interaction between independent variables. Additionally, write up the three results as they would be printed in a journal article or report (see page 251 of the text for a reference). The dependent variable consists of health scores, while the independent variables consist of gender and social class. In regard to health scores, higher values indicate better overall physical health.

    Note: Include both independent variables as fixed factors.

Health Score	Gender	Social Class
98	Female	Upper
88	Male	Upper
87	Female	Upper
85	Female	Middle
75	Female	Upper
74	Male	Upper
72	Male	Middle
71	Female	Middle
65	Male	Middle
55	Male	Upper
47	Male	Middle
33	Male	Lower
22	Female	Lower
10	Male	Upper
5	Male	Lower

Just for fun/Challenge yourself

1. Using the following data, conduct a multivariate analysis of variance in SPSS and interpret the results. The two dependent variables are health scores and lifestyle attitudes. Higher values on the health score variable indicate better general physical health, while higher scores on the lifestyle attitudes variable indicate more positive and more healthy attitudes.

Lifestyle Attitudes	Health Score	Gender	Social Class
88	98	Female	Upper
76	88	Male	Upper
98	87	Female	Upper
76	85	Female	Middle
67	75	Female	Upper
86	74	Male	Upper
65	72	Male	Middle
67	71	Female	Middle
65	65	Male	Middle
43	55	Male	Upper
54	47	Male	Middle
22	33	Male	Lower
32	22	Female	Lower
11	10	Male	Upper
2	5	Male	Lower

True/False questions
1. False. The factorial analysis of variance can be used when you have two, or more than two, independent/treatment variables.
2. False. Whether the interaction effects are significant will not depend on whether the main effects are significant or not.

Multiple choice questions
1. c. You have two independent variables, and participants are tested only once
2. c. The number of main effects will be equal to the number of interaction effects
3. a. An interaction effect
4. b. Lines that cross/are not parallel

Exercises
1. This first graph presents an example of a strong interaction effect, as illustrated by the lines that cross and have very different slopes, or directions:

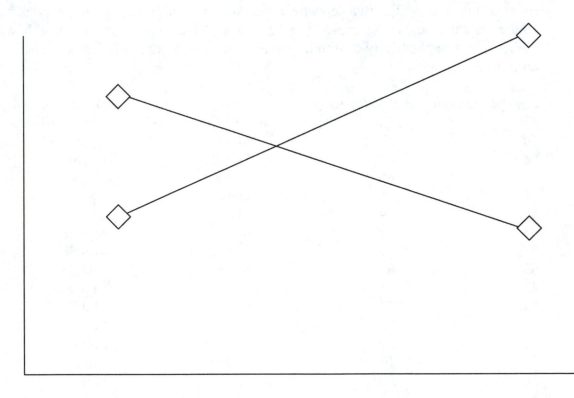

This next graph is illustrative of no interaction effect, as the lines are exactly parallel to each other:

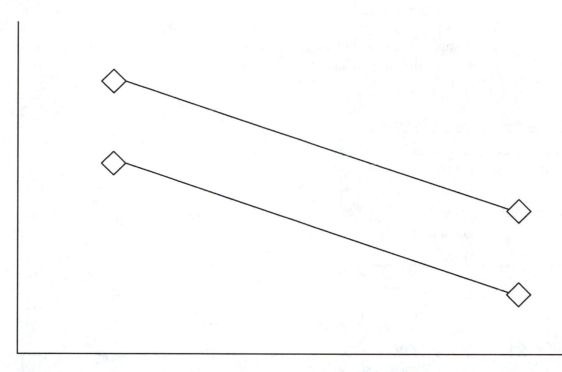

Short-answer/essay questions

1. A factorial ANOVA would be preferred over a one-way ANOVA whenever there is more than one independent, or treatment variable. The factorial ANOVA would be preferred because the one-way ANOVA can only incorporate a single independent variable into the analysis.

SPSS Questions

1. The eight steps of hypothesis testing are presented here:

    1. State the null and research hypotheses:

        The null hypotheses:
        For gender: H_0: $\mu_{male} = \mu_{female}$
        For social class: H_0: $\mu_{upper} = \mu_{middle} = \mu_{lower}$
        For the interaction effect: $\mu_{upper \bullet male} = \mu_{upper \bullet female} = \mu_{middle \bullet male} = \mu_{middle \bullet female} = \mu_{lower \bullet male} = \mu_{lower \bullet female}$

        The research hypotheses:
        For gender: H_1: $\overline{X}_{male} \neq \overline{X}_{female}$

        For social class: H_1: $\overline{X}_{upper} \neq \overline{X}_{middle} \neq \overline{X}_{lower}$
        For the interaction effect:
        $\overline{X}_{upper \bullet male} \neq \overline{X}_{upper \bullet female} \neq \overline{X}_{middle \bullet male} \neq \overline{X}_{middle \bullet female} \neq \overline{X}_{lower \bullet male} \neq \overline{X}_{lower \bullet female}$

99

2. Set the level of significance: 0.05
3. Select the appropriate test statistic: A factorial ANOVA
4. Compute the test statistic value: The SPSS output relating to this test is presented in the following tables:

Between-Subjects Factors

		N
Gender	Female	6
	Male	9
Social_Class	Lower	3
	Middle	5
	Upper	7

Tests of Between-Subjects Effects

Dependent Variable:Health_Score

Source	Type III Sum of Squares	df	Mean Square	F	Sig.
Corrected Model	7623.650[a]	5	1524.730	3.016	.072
Intercept	35936.250	1	35936.250	71.081	.000
Gender	842.917	1	842.917	1.667	.229
Social_Class	5517.382	2	2758.691	5.457	.028
Gender * Social_Class	373.808	2	186.904	.370	.701
Error	4550.083	9	505.565		
Total	64625.000	15			
Corrected Total	12173.733	14			

a. R Squared = .626 (Adjusted R Squared = .419)

5. Determine the value needed for rejection of the null hypothesis: This step is automatically done by SPSS, so does not need to be done manually.
6. Compare the obtained value and the critical value: This step can be completed by looking at the significance values for the main and interaction effects as presented in the previous table. As we can see, the main effect of gender is not significant while the main effect of social class is. Additionally, the interaction between gender and social class was not found to be significant.
7. & 8. Decisions: The null hypothesis that there is no difference in health scores on the basis of gender cannot be rejected, as the main effect was not found to be significant. Additionally, the null hypothesis that stated there was no interaction effect between gender and social class can also not be rejected, as this interaction effect was also not found to be significant. However, the null hypothesis suggesting no difference in health scores on the basis of social class can be

rejected, as this main effect was found to be significant. This suggests that while there is no difference in health scores on the basis of gender, and no interaction between gender and social class, there is a significant difference in health scores on the basis of social class.

Also, as might be seen in a journal article, these three results could be written up in the following way:

Gender: $F_{(1,9)} = 1.67, p = .229$
Social class: $F_{(2,9)} = 5.46, p < .05$
Interaction between gender and social class: $F_{(2,9)} = 0.37, p = .701$

Just for fun/Challenge yourself
1. Using the following data, conduct a multivariate analysis of variance in SPSS and interpret the results. The two dependent variables are health scores and lifestyle attitudes.

These results are presented in the following tables:

Between-Subjects Factors

		N
Gender	Female	6
	Male	9
Social_Class	Lower	3
	Middle	5
	Upper	7

Multivariate Tests[c]

Effect		Value	F	Hypothesis df	Error df	Sig.
Intercept	Pillai's Trace	.892	33.155[a]	2.000	8.000	.000
	Wilks' Lambda	.108	33.155[a]	2.000	8.000	.000
	Hotelling's Trace	8.289	33.155[a]	2.000	8.000	.000
	Roy's Largest Root	8.289	33.155[a]	2.000	8.000	.000
Gender	Pillai's Trace	.238	1.251[a]	2.000	8.000	.337
	Wilks' Lambda	.762	1.251[a]	2.000	8.000	.337
	Hotelling's Trace	.313	1.251[a]	2.000	8.000	.337
	Roy's Largest Root	.313	1.251[a]	2.000	8.000	.337
Social_Class	Pillai's Trace	.552	1.717	4.000	18.000	.190
	Wilks' Lambda	.449	1.969[a]	4.000	16.000	.148

	Hotelling's Trace	1.223	2.140	4.000	14.000	.130
	Roy's Largest Root	1.220	5.490[b]	2.000	9.000	.028
Gender * Social_Class	Pillai's Trace	.286	.751	4.000	18.000	.570
	Wilks' Lambda	.727	.690[a]	4.000	16.000	.610
	Hotelling's Trace	.356	.623	4.000	14.000	.654
	Roy's Largest Root	.293	1.319[b]	2.000	9.000	.314

a. Exact statistic

b. The statistic is an upper bound on F that yields a lower bound on the significance level.

c. Design: Intercept + Gender + Social_Class + Gender * Social_Class

Tests of Between-Subjects Effects

Source	Dependent Variable	Type III Sum of Squares	df	Mean Square	F	Sig.
Corrected Model	Lifestyle_Attitudes	7428.567[a]	5	1485.713	3.110	.066
	Health_Score	7623.650[b]	5	1524.730	3.016	.072
Intercept	Lifestyle_Attitudes	34056.010	1	34056.010	71.283	.000
	Health_Score	35936.250	1	35936.250	71.081	.000
Gender	Lifestyle_Attitudes	1254.943	1	1254.943	2.627	.140
	Health_Score	842.917	1	842.917	1.667	.229
Social_Class	Lifestyle_Attitudes	4620.377	2	2310.188	4.835	.037
	Health_Score	5517.382	2	2758.691	5.457	.028
Gender * Social_Class	Lifestyle_Attitudes	289.313	2	144.656	.303	.746
	Health_Score	373.808	2	186.904	.370	.701
Error	Lifestyle_Attitudes	4299.833	9	477.759		
	Health_Score	4550.083	9	505.565		
Total	Lifestyle_Attitudes	60122.000	15			
	Health_Score	64625.000	15			
Corrected Total	Lifestyle_Attitudes	11728.400	14			
	Health_Score	12173.733	14			

a. R Squared = .633 (Adjusted R Squared = .430)

b. R Squared = .626 (Adjusted R Squared = .419)

Focusing on the final table, these results suggest that social class is a significant predictor of both health scores as well as lifestyle attitudes, while neither gender nor the interaction between gender and social class significantly predict either of these two dependent variables.

Chapter 15: Cousins or Just Good Friends? Testing Relationships Using the Correlation Coefficient

Chapter outline
- Introduction to Testing the Correlation Coefficient
  - The Path to Wisdom and Knowledge
- Computing the Test Statistic
  - So How Do I Interpret $r_{(27)} = .393$, $p < .05$?
  - Causes and Associations (Again!)
  - Significance Versus Meaningfulness (Again, Again!)
- Using the Computer to Compute a Correlation Coefficient (Again)
  - What the SPSS Output Means
- Summary
- Time to Practice

Learning objectives
- Learn how to test for the significance of a correlation coefficient and how to interpret the results.
- Review the difference between significance and causality in relation to correlation coefficients.
- Review the difference between significance and meaningfulness.
- Learn how to use SPSS to calculate the significance of a correlation coefficient.

Summary/key points
- This chapter covers correlation coefficients, which was discussed earlier in the text, but this chapter also covers the use of statistical significance in relation to correlation coefficients.
  - Correlation coefficients examine the relationship between variables, not the difference between groups.
  - A correlation coefficient can only test two variables at a time.
  - The appropriate test statistic to use is the t test for the correlation coefficient
  - Tests can be either directional or nondirectional
- A significant correlation does not indicate causality.
- A significant correlation does not necessarily indicate a meaningful relationship.

Key terms
{Omitted: No new terms are included in this section}

True/False questions
1. The correlation coefficient can only be used for two-tailed tests.
2. A significant correlation between two variables does not imply that one variable causes the other.

3. A significant correlation also indicates a meaningful relationship between the two variables included in the analysis.

Multiple choice questions
1. The correlation coefficient examines:
    a. Differences between two groups
    b. Differences between two or more groups
    c. The relationship between two variables
    d. The relationship between two or more variables
2. In the case of the correlation coefficient, the appropriate test statistic to use is:
    a. The F test for the correlation coefficient
    b. The t test for the correlation coefficient
    c. The p test for the correlation coefficient
    d. The r test for the correlation coefficient
3. Which of the following results is significant at the .05 level (two-tailed)?
    a. $r_{(30)} = .33$
    b. $r_{(60)} = .24$
    c. $r_{(4)} = .79$
    d. $r_{(10)} = .59$
4. Which of the following results is significant at the .01 level (one-tailed)?
    a. $r_{(30)} = .42$
    b. $r_{(10)} = .62$
    c. $r_{(4)} = .87$
    d. $r_{(5)} = .81$

Exercises
{Omitted: See SPSS section}

Short-answer/essay questions
1. What is the critical value of the correlation coefficient needed for rejection of the null hypothesis if your degrees of freedom is 15 and you are conducting a one-tailed test using the .01 level of significance?
2. What is the critical value of the correlation coefficient needed for rejection of the null hypothesis if your degrees of freedom is 30 and you are conducting a two-tailed test using the .05 level of significance?
3. If your total sample size is 75, what is your degrees of freedom for the correlation coefficient?
4. Your degrees of freedom is 55. Looking at the table of critical values for the correlation coefficient, you can see that there are only entries for 50 and 60 degrees of freedom, not 55. If you want to be more conservative, which entry should you choose?
5. How would you interpret $r_{(37)} = .89, p < .05$?

1. Using SPSS, perform the eight steps of hypothesis testing to test the null hypothesis that there is no relationship between IQ and salary, using the following set of data. Also, report your result in the following form: $r_{(17)} = .55, p < .05$.

Salary ($1000)	IQ
245	127
120	133
90	98
88	105
75	115
74	102
66	115
58	98
45	80
23	85
21	78
15	70

Just for fun/Challenge yourself

1. Why do the critical values for the correlation coefficient decrease as the sample size increases? Why do they increase when you have a lower value for the possibility of Type I error?

Answer key

True/False questions

1. False. The correlation coefficient can be used for both one-tailed and two-tailed tests.
2. True.
3. False. You can have a significant correlation that is very weak, meaning that there is a very weak relationship (hence, not meaningful) between the two variables.

Multiple choice questions

1. c. The relationship between two variables
2. b. The t test for the correlation coefficient
3. d. $r_{(10)} = .59$
4. a. $r_{(30)} = .42$

Exercises
{Omitted: See SPSS section}

Short-answer/essay questions
1. The critical value is .5577
2. The critical value is .3494
3. The degrees of freedom = n - 2 = 75 - 2 = 73
4. To be more conservative, you choose the entry for 50 degrees of freedom, which results in a higher critical value for the correlation coefficient, making the test more conservative, or more difficult to be found significant.
5. First, r represents the test statistic that was used. 37 is the number of degrees of freedom. .89 represents the obtained value that was calculated for the correlation coefficient. Finally, $p < .05$ indicates the probability is less than 5% that the relationship between the two variables is due to chance alone. We can conclude that there is a significant relationship between the two variables included in the analysis.

SPSS Questions
1. The eight steps are presented here:
    1. State the null and research hypotheses:
       $H_0: \rho_{xy} = 0$
       $H_1: r_{xy} \neq 0$
    2. Set the level of significance: .05
    3. Select the appropriate statistic: The correlation coefficient
    4. Compute the test statistic value: This is done for us automatically in SPSS. The following table illustrates the SPSS output.

Correlations

		Salary_1k	IQ
Salary_1k	Pearson Correlation	1	.772**
	Sig. (2-tailed)		.003
	N	12	12
IQ	Pearson Correlation	.772**	1
	Sig. (2-tailed)	.003	
	N	12	12

**. Correlation is significant at the 0.01 level (2-tailed).

5. Determine the value needed for rejection of the null hypothesis: As our sample size is 12, we know that our degrees of freedom is 10. As we are conducting a two-tailed test using the .05 level of significance, our critical value would be .5760. Note: This step does not necessarily need to be done as SPSS automatically calculates the significance level for the correlation coefficient.
6. Compare the obtained value with the critical value: Our obtained value is higher than our critical value.

7. & 8. Decisions: As our obtained value is higher than our critical value, you can reject the null hypothesis that there is no relationship between IQ and salary. As we obtained a positive correlation coefficient, this indicates that there is a positive association between these two variables, meaning that higher IQ is associated with higher salary.

Additionally, this result can be reported as: $r_{(10)} = .772$, $p < .05$.

Just for fun/Challenge yourself
1. Critical values for the correlation coefficient (and, more generally) decrease as the sample size increases because as we have a greater number of individuals, it is easier for a relationship of a certain strength to be seen - hence, when you have a lot of data, you don't need a very strong relationship in order to achieve statistical significance. On the other hand, when your sample size is very small, the correlation coefficient must be very high for you to be able to say that the relationship is valid, and not just due to chance. Additionally, a lower value for the probability of Type I error means that you have a higher degree of certainty that the relationship is valid, and not due to chance. Therefore, your correlation coefficient must be that much higher in order to have a greater degree of certainty.

Chapter 16: Predicting Who'll Win the Super Bowl: Using Linear Regression

Chapter outline
- What Is Prediction All About?
- The Logic of Prediction
- Drawing the World's Best Line (for Your Data)
  - How Good Is Our Prediction?
- Using the Computer to Compute the Regression Line
  - What the SPSS Output Means
- The More Predictors the Better? Maybe
  - The Big Rule(s) When It Comes to Using Multiple Predictor Variables
- Summary
- Time to Practice

Learning objectives
- Learn about linear regression and how it can be used for prediction.
- Understand when it is appropriate to use linear regression.
- Learn how to determine the accuracy of your predictions.
- Understand when it is and when it is not appropriate to include multiple independent variables in a linear regression.

Summary/key points
- Linear regression, in essence, uses correlations between variables as the basis for the prediction of the value of one variable based on the value of another.
  - The higher the absolute value of the correlation coefficient, the more accurate the prediction is of one variable based on the other variable.
    - A perfect correlation would translate into perfect prediction in the case of linear regression.
  - In linear regression, a regression equation is determined, which can be used to plot a regression line. The regression line reflects the best estimate of predicted scores for the dependent variable based on levels of the independent variable.
    - In the regression equation, the predicted score of the dependent variable is equal to the slope multiplied by the value of the independent variable, plus a constant which is equal to the point at which the regression line crosses the y-axis.
  - Error in prediction (error of estimate) is calculated as the distance between each individual data point and the regression line - this figure illustrates by how much your prediction was "off".
    - Standard error of estimate is computed as the average of all values for error in prediction. This value tells you how much imprecision there is overall in regard to the predictive power of the linear regression analysis.
    - Error will decrease as the correlation between the two variables increases.
- In linear regression, the outcome variable is called the criterion or dependent variable, indicated as Y, while the predictor or independent variable is indicated as X.

- Multiple regression consists of a type of regression in which more than one independent variable is included in the analysis.
  - Additional independent variables should only be included if they make a unique contribution to the understanding, or prediction, of the dependent variable.
  - Additionally, when including multiple independent variables in a regression analysis, it is best if they are uncorrelated with one another, but are both correlated to the dependent variable.

Key terms
- Regression equation: In regression, an equation that defines the line that has the best fit with your data.
- Regression line: The line of best fit that is drawn (or calculated) based on the values in the regression equation.
- Line of best fit: The regression line that best fits the data and minimizes the error in prediction.
- Error in prediction (a.k.a. Error of estimate): The difference between the actual score and the predicted score in a regression.
- Criterion or dependent variable: The outcome variable, or the variable that is predicted in a regression analysis.
- Predictor or independent variable: The variable that is used to predict the dependent variable in a regression analysis.
- Y prime: The predicted value of Y, the dependent variable.
- Standard error of estimate: The average amount that each data point differs from the predicted data point.
- Multiple regression: A type of regression in which more than one independent variable is included in the analysis.

True/False questions
1. Linear regression uses correlations as its basis.
2. Linear regression can be used to predict values on the dependent variable for individuals outside of your data set.
3. The higher the absolute value of your correlation coefficient, the worse your predictive power will be.
4. When using multiple linear regression, it is always best to include as many predictor variables as possible.
5. When using multiple linear regression, it is best to select independent variables that are uncorrelated with one another, but are all related to the predicted variable.

Multiple choice questions
1. Your prediction in linear regression will be perfect if your correlation is:
   a. -1
   b. +1
   c. 0

     d. Either a. or b.
2. If the prediction was perfect, all predicted points would fall:
     a. On the regression line
     b. Above the regression line
     c. Below the regression line
     d. Both above and below the regression line
3. If your standard error of estimate is high, this means that the plot of the regression line with data points would show:
     a. Data points very close to the regression line
     b. Data points very far from the regression line
     c. Data points exactly on the regression line
     d. This cannot be determined on the basis of this information
4. The variable that is predicted in linear regression is called:
     a. The criterion variable
     b. The dependent variable
     c. The predictor variable
     d. The independent variable
     e. Both a. and b.
5. The variable that is used to predict another variable in linear regression is called:
     a. The criterion variable
     b. The dependent variable
     c. The predicted variable
     c. The independent variable
6. In linear regression, the dependent variable is indicated by:
     a. Y
     b. b
     c. X
     d. a
7. In linear regression, the independent variable is indicated by:
     a. Y
     b. b
     c. X
     d. a
8. In linear regression, the slope is indicated by:
     a. Y
     b. b
     c. X
     d. a
9. In linear regression, the point at which the line crosses the y-axis is indicated by:
     a. Y
     b. b
     c. X
     d. a
10. The predicted value of Y is called:
     a. Y prime
     b. Y sigma

     c. Y delta

     d. Y alpha

11. In linear regression, the regression line can be...
     a. A straight line only
     b. A straight or curved line
     c. A curved line only
     d. None of the above

12. If you have a correlation coefficient of -1, the standard error of estimate will be equal to the following:
     a. 1
     b. -1
     c. 2
     d. 0

Exercises

1. Using the following data, conduct a linear regression analysis (by hand). In this analysis, you are testing whether SAT scores are predictive of overall college GPA. Also, write out the regression equation. How would you interpret your results?

SAT score	GPA
670	1.2
720	1.8
750	2.3
845	1.9
960	3.0
1000	3.3
1180	3.2
1200	3.4
1370	2.9
1450	3.8
1580	4.0
1600	3.9

2. You conduct a linear regression in which the number of hours per week spent exercising is used to predict the respondent's overall general health, measured on a scale from 0 to 100 with 100 being the best possible health. You obtain the following results: $b = 4.5$, $a = 37$. Using the general formula for the regression line, calculate the predicted values for the respondent's overall general health for respondents who spend 0 hours per week exercising, 3 hours per week exercising, and 12 hours per week exercising.

Short-answer/essay questions
{Omitted}

1. Using the data presented under the "Exercises" section, Question 1, conduct the same linear regression using SPSS and interpret the output. Additionally, create a scatterplot of the data with a superimposed regression line.

Just for fun/Challenge yourself
1. Using the data from the "Exercises" section, question 2, you find two new individuals who have a health score of 100 and 75, respectively. Calculate their predicted values for the number of hours they exercise per week.
2. Using the following data, conduct a multiple linear regression in SPSS and interpret the results. SAT score and IQ are both independent variables, and GRE score is the dependent variable. Interpret the results and write out the regression equation.

SAT score	IQ	GPA
670	80	1.2
720	87	1.8
750	105	2.3
845	95	1.9
960	110	3.0
1000	98	3.3
1180	110	3.2
1200	125	3.4
1370	115	2.9
1450	120	3.8
1580	140	4.0
1600	135	3.9

Answer key

True/False questions
1. True.
2. True.
3. False. The higher the absolute value of your correlation coefficient, the better your predictive power will be.
4. False. Careful judgment should be used when deciding on what predictor variables to include.
5. True.

Multiple choice questions
1. d. Either a. or b.
3. a. On the regression line
4. b. Data points very far from the regression line
5. e. Both a. and b.

6. d. The independent variable
6. a. Y
7. c. X
8. b. b
9. d. a
10. a. Y prime
11. a. A straight line only
12. d. 0

Exercises

1. The regression coefficients would be calculated using the following equations:

$$b = \frac{\sum XY - \left(\sum X \sum Y / n\right)}{\sum X^2 - \left[\left(\sum X\right)^2 / n\right]} = \frac{41509.5 - \left(13325 \bullet 34.7 / 12\right)}{16033625 - \left[\left(13325\right)^2 / 12\right]} = 0.002$$

$$a = \frac{\sum Y - b \sum X}{n} = \frac{34.7 - .002 \bullet 13325}{12} = 0.219$$

The regression equation would be represented as:

$$Y' = .002X + .219$$

The value for *a*, .219, indicates the predicted GPA if the SAT score was equal to zero. The value for *b*, .002, indicates that a one unit increase in SAT score is associated with a .002 predicted increase in GPA. Multiplying this figure by 100, we can say that a 100 unit increase in SAT score is associated with a 0.2 predicted increase in GPA. This means, more generally, that higher SAT scores are associated with higher GPAs.

2. The regression equation would be:

$$Y' = 4.5X + 37$$

For respondents who spend 0 hours per week exercising:

$$Y' = 4.5(0) + 37 = 37$$

For respondents who spend 3 hours per week exercising:

$$Y' = 4.5(3) + 37 = 40.5$$

For respondents who spend 12 hours per week exercising:

$$Y' = 4.5(12) + 37 = 81$$

Short-answer/essay questions
{Omitted}

SPSS Questions
1. The SPSS output is shown here:

Model Summary

Model	R	R Square	Adjusted R Square	Std. Error of the Estimate
1	.893[a]	.797	.777	.42679

a. Predictors: (Constant), SAT

ANOVA[b]

Model		Sum of Squares	df	Mean Square	F	Sig.
1	Regression	7.168	1	7.168	39.351	.000[a]
	Residual	1.821	10	.182		
	Total	8.989	11			

a. Predictors: (Constant), SAT

b. Dependent Variable: GPA

Coefficients[a]

Model		Unstandardized Coefficients		Standardized Coefficients	t	Sig.
		B	Std. Error	Beta		
1	(Constant)	.219	.444		.494	.632
	SAT	.002	.000	.893	6.273	.000

a. Dependent Variable: GPA

The final *Coefficients* table gives us our *a* and *b* values.

The value for *a*, .219, indicates the predicted GPA if the SAT score was equal to zero. The value for *b*, .002, indicates that a one unit increase in SAT score is associated with a .002 predicted increase in GPA. Multiplying this figure by 100, we can say that a 100 unit increase in SAT score is associated with a 0.2 predicted increase in GPA. This means, more generally, that higher SAT scores are associated with higher GPAs. Additionally, the effect of SAT was found to be significant at the .05 level of significance.

The scatter plot with superimposed regression line is shown here:

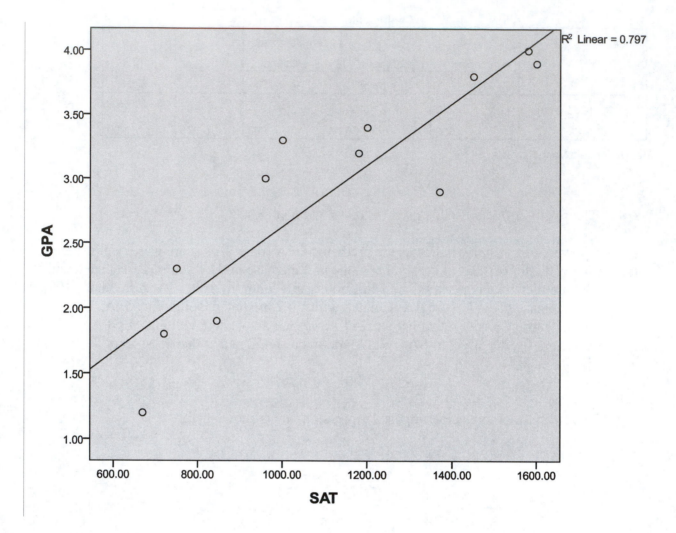

Just for fun/Challenge yourself

1. The results were: b = 4.5, a = 37

   Giving us: $Y' = 4.5X + 37$

   If a respondent had a health score of 100:

   $Y' = 4.5X + 37 \rightarrow 100 = 4.5X + 37 \rightarrow 63 = 4.5X \rightarrow X = 14$

   If a respondent had a health score of 75:

   $Y' = 4.5X + 37 \rightarrow 75 = 4.5X + 37 \rightarrow 38 = 4.5X \rightarrow X = 8.44$

2. The SPSS output is shown here:

Model Summary

Model	R	R Square	Adjusted R Square	Std. Error of the Estimate
1	.917[a]	.841	.805	.39901

a. Predictors: (Constant), IQ, SAT

ANOVA[b]

Model		Sum of Squares	df	Mean Square	F	Sig.
1	Regression	7.556	2	3.778	23.731	.000[a]
	Residual	1.433	9	.159		
	Total	8.989	11			

a. Predictors: (Constant), IQ, SAT

b. Dependent Variable: GPA

Coefficients[a]

Model		Unstandardized Coefficients		Standardized Coefficients	t	Sig.
		B	Std. Error	Beta		
1	(Constant)	-1.144	.966		-1.184	.267
	SAT	.001	.001	.432	1.334	.215
	IQ	.025	.016	.506	1.562	.153

a. Dependent Variable: GPA

Neither SAT nor IQ were found to be significant. However, based on the coefficients, a one unit increase in SAT was associated with a .001 unit increase in GPA, while a one unit increase in IQ was associated with a .025 unit increase in GPA. The value for a, -1.144, indicates the predicted GPA if the SAT score and IQ was equal to zero.

The regression equation would be:

$$Y' = .001(SAT) + .025(IQ) + -1.144$$

Chapter 17: What to Do When You're Not Normal: Chi-Square and Some Other Non-Parametric Tests

Chapter outline
- Introduction to Nonparametric Statistics
- Introduction to One-Sample Chi-Square
- Computing the Chi-Square Test Statistic
  - So How Do I Interpret $\chi^2_{(2)} = 20.6, p < .05$?
- Using the Computer to Perform a Chi-Square Test
  - What the SPSS Output Means
- Other Nonparametric Tests You Should Know about
- Summary
- Time to Practice

Learning objectives
- Understand the reason behind the use of nonparametric statistics and when they should be preferred.
- Learn about chi-square and how it is calculated, both by hand and using SPSS.
- Briefly review some other nonparametric statistics.

Summary/key points
- The statistical tests covered previously in this book consisted of parametric statistical tests, which include certain assumptions about the data, sample size, etc.
- Nonparametric statistics do not incorporate these same assumptions. These types of statistics can be utilized when the assumptions of parametric statistical tests have been violated.
  - Nonparametric statistics can be preferred when you have sample sizes that are very small (less than 30) or are analyzing categorical variables.
- Chi-square is the nonparametric test highlighted in this chapter.
  - A one sample chi-square focuses on the distribution of a single variable. It is used to determine whether the distribution of a single categorical variable is significantly different from that which would be expected by chance.
    - The one sample chi-square test is also called goodness of fit.
  - A two sample chi-square focuses on the relationship between two categorical variables. It determines whether the variables are significantly related, or dependent.
  - The chi-square statistic measures the difference between the observed data and what would be expected by chance alone.

Key terms
- Parametric statistics: A set of statistical tests which incorporate certain assumptions.

- Nonparametric statistics (a.k.a. Distribution-free statistics): A set of statistical tests which do not incorporate the assumptions held by parametric statistical tests.
- Chi-square: A nonparametric statistical test used to determine whether a single variable has a distribution that would be expected through chance, or whether there is a general relationship between two categorical variables.

True/False questions
1. Nonparametric statistics include more assumptions than parametric statistics.
2. Chi-square is a nonparametric statistical test.

Multiple choice questions
1. This test is also known as goodness of fit:
    a. One-sample chi-square
    b. Two-sample chi-square
    c. Any nonparametric statistical test
    d. Fisher's exact test
2. This test is used to determine whether the distribution of a single categorical variable significantly differs from that which would be expected by chance:
    a. Two-sample chi-square
    b. Fisher's exact test
    c. Kolmogorov-Smirnov test
    d. One-sample chi-square
3. This test is used to determine whether two categorical variables are related, or dependent:
    a. Two-sample chi-square
    b. The sign test
    c. Kolmogorov-Smirnov test
    d. One-sample chi-square
4. Nonparametric statistics might be preferred when:
    a. Your sample size is very small
    b. Your sample size is vary large
    c. The variables you are analyzing are continuous
    d. All the assumptions of parametric statistics have been met
5. When calculating the chi-square statistic, if there is no difference between what is observed and what is expected, your chi-square value will be:
    a. 1
    b. 0
    c. -1
    d. It is impossible to determine this given the information
6. Which of the following values is significant at the .05 level?
    a. $\chi^2_{(10)} = 15.43$
    b. $\chi^2_{(8)} = 12.20$
    c. $\chi^2_{(5)} = 11.12$

$$\chi^2_{(2)} = 4.23$$

d.

7. Which of the following values is significant at the .01 level?

    a. $\chi^2_{(12)} = 22.14$

    b. $\chi^2_{(6)} = 14.20$

    c. $\chi^2_{(4)} = 8.42$

    d. $\chi^2_{(2)} = 9.45$

Exercises

1. Using the following data, perform the eight steps of hypothesis testing. In this question, calculate the chi-square statistic by hand.

Expected number	Observed number
10	15
20	15
20	37
50	33

Short-answer/essay questions

1. Interpret the following: $\chi^2_{(3)} = 14.2, p < .05$

SPSS Questions

1. Using the following data, perform a chi-square analysis using SPSS. Interpret your results.

Expected number	Observed number
10	8
10	10
10	11
10	9

Just for fun/Challenge yourself

1. What test can be used to see if scores from a sample come from a specified population?
2. Which test computes the exact probability of outcomes in a 2x2 table?
3. Which test computes the correlation between ranks?

True/False questions
1. False. Nonparametric statistics include fewer assumptions than parametric statistics.
2. True.

Multiple choice questions
1. a. One-sample chi-square
2. d. One-sample chi-square
3. a. Two-sample chi-square
4. a. Your sample size is very small
5. b. 0
6. c. $\chi^2_{(5)} = 11.12$
7. d. $\chi^2_{(2)} = 9.45$

Exercises
1. The eight steps of hypothesis testing are presented here:

    1. State the null and research hypotheses:
        H_0: $P_1 = P_2 = P_3 = P_4$
        H_1: $P_1 \neq P_2 \neq P_3 \neq P_4$

    2. Set the level of significance: 0.05
    3. Select the appropriate test statistic: Chi-square
    4. Compute the test statistic value:

Expected number	Observed number
10	15
20	15
20	37
50	33

        $$\chi^2 = \sum \frac{(O-E)^2}{E} = \frac{(15-10)^2}{10} + \frac{(15-20)^2}{20} + \frac{(37-20)^2}{20} + \frac{(33-50)^2}{50} = 23.98$$

    5. Determine the value needed to reject the null hypothesis: Critical $\chi^2 = 7.82$
    6. Compare the obtained value with the critical value: The obtained value, 23.98, is larger than the critical value of 7.82.
    7. & 8. Decision: As the obtained value is greater than the critical value, we would reject the null hypothesis that there is no difference between these groups.

Short-answer/essay questions

1. First, χ^2 (chi-square) represents the test statistic. The value of three represents the degrees of freedom, while 14.2 is the obtained value arrived at by using the formula for chi-square. Finally, $p < .05$ indicates that the probability is less than 5% that the variable is equally distributed across all categories.

SPSS Questions

1. The SPSS output is shown in the following table. The results indicate that this test did not find statistical significance, meaning that the distribution of the variable cannot be said to significantly differ from that expected through chance alone.

Test Statistics

	Var1
Chi-square	.600[a]
Df	3
Asymp. Sig.	.896

a. 0 cells (.0%) have expected frequencies less than 5. The minimum expected cell frequency is 10.0.

Just for fun/Challenge yourself

1. The Kolmogorov-Smirnov test
2. Fisher's exact test
3. The Spearman rank correlation coefficient

Chapter 18: Some Other (Important) Statistical Procedures You Should Know about

Chapter outline
- Multivariate Analysis of Variance
- Repeated Measures Analysis of Variance
- Analysis of Covariance
- Multiple Regression
- Factor Analysis
- Path Analysis
- Structural Equation Modeling
- Summary

Learning objectives
- Review some more advanced statistical procedures and when and how they are used.

Summary/key points
- This chapter presents an overview of some more advanced statistical tests.
- MANOVA (Multiple Analysis of Variance) is used when you want to include more than one dependent variable in an analysis. This can be preferred as when the dependent variables are related to one another, it is difficult to determine the effect of the treatment or independent variable on any one outcome.
- Repeated measures analysis of variance is used when there is one factor on which participants are tested more than once.
- Analysis of covariance is used when you want to control for the effect of one or more continuous variables.
- Multiple regression is a type of linear regression which includes more than one independent variable.
- Factor analysis is used to determine how closely related a set of items are and how they might form clusters or factors. This can be preferred as factors can be better at representing outcomes than individual variables.
- Path analysis studies causality between variables.
- Structural equation modeling (SEM) is an extension of path analysis and is also considered a generalization of regression and factor analysis. SEM is considered confirmatory as opposed to exploratory.